HOW WE GOT
THE BIBLE

by

Neil R. Lightfoot

BAKER BOOK HOUSE
Grand Rapids, Michigan

Library of Congress Catalog Number: 62-22230

Copyright, 1963, by
NEIL R. LIGHTFOOT

ISBN: 0-8010-5502-4

First Printing, January 1963
Second Printing, August 1963
Third Printing, May 1965
Fourth Printing, September 1966
Fifth Printing, August 1968
Sixth Printing, September 1970
Seventh Printing, October 1972

PHOTOLITHOPRINTED BY CUSHING - MALLOY, INC.
ANN ARBOR, MICHIGAN, UNITED STATES OF AMERICA
1972

To Ollie, my wife

Foreword

This study seeks to be a factual and honest account of how the Bible has been preserved and handed down to our generation. The subject is vast and at times complex. It has been my constant aim, therefore, to simplify the material and to state it, so far as possible, in a non-technical manner. On the other hand, I have tried to get down to the heart of the question, for too many studies of this kind have been content with the mere citing of superficial facts about the Bible. These facts are important and interesting, of course, but they do not tell us *how* we got the Bible.

At first this book was planned and written as a series of lessons for adult Bible classes. In the present edition the original publication has been expanded somewhat, but most of the basic material remains unchanged. This means that the extent of the study and its objects have been necessarily limited. Possibly this will account, in part at least, for the obvious shortcomings of the effort. But if there is anything in particular to commend it, perhaps it will prove helpful to the person who has little background in these subjects and little time to pursue them in detail.

Although this edition is designed for the average reader, it is hoped that it will be useful for general Bible classes as well. If so, the teacher who leads in the study may find his task difficult. It will indeed be difficult unless due care and thought are given to each point. The teacher perhaps will wish to supplement the material by additional reading of selected books and articles in Bible dictionaries and encyclopedias. Two current books which are especially recommended are *Our Bible and the Ancient Manuscripts,* by Sir Frederic Kenyon (revised by A. W. Adams), and *The Books and the Parchments,* by F. F. Bruce.

It should be noted, in conclusion, that some of these chapters comprise a unit of study. For example, Chapters 5, 6 and 7 form a group and should not be isolated from each other. It is likely that this group will present more difficulty than any other part of the study. Thus these chapters, along with others, should be read and re-read. It is hoped that this will not prove to be tedious, but rather will enrich us in our understanding and appreciation of the Sacred Word which is able to instruct us for salvation.

Neil R. Lightfoot

Abilene Christian College
October, 1962

Contents

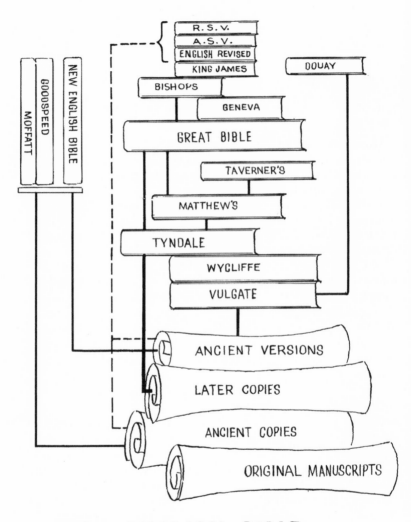

THE ENGLISH BIBLE

1

The Making of Ancient Books

How the Bible has come down to us is a story of adventure and devotion. It is a story of toil and faith by those who, sometimes at great cost, passed down from generation to generation the message of salvation. The Bible did not just happen nor has it been preserved through the years by mere chance. The Bible is a marvel all its own. Living in a day when books are written and printed by thousands we are apt to overlook the fascinating drama that lies behind our Bible. How and when did the books of the Bible have their origin? In what sense are these books different from other books? How have these books been preserved and transmitted to us? These are some of the questions that arise in the mind of every thoughtful student of the Bible; and the answers to these questions compose a story which spans thousands of years, that takes us to various regions of the world and into the hearts of countless unnamed people whose first love was the Word of God.

The starting-point of our Bible is preceded and determined by another story, the history of ancient books and writing. It is necessary to know this story because the Bible is composed of documents which were not only written long ago, but have been transmitted and preserved through the years by means of writing. To know then something of the early history of writing and the origin of ancient books will provide an interesting background for the history of the Bible and at the same time will contribute immeasurably to the understanding of the life-situations in which the Word of God had its birth. Thus the whole history of the Bible is conditioned upon (1) the history of writing, and (2) the history of the materials used in the making of ancient books.

Early Writing and the Materials Used

Our Bible is a very old book, but it is by no means the oldest book in the world. Discoveries made within the last century show that writing was a well-established art in many countries long before the beginnings of the Hebrew nation in the land of Palestine. The earliest known examples of writing carry us into the ancient land of Egypt where inscriptions have been found which date as far back as 4000-5000 B.C. In Babylonia inscriptions are extant of king Sargon I who lived about 3750 B.C., and the writings of the Sumerians of this area date back even earlier. In Palestine itself letters written by governors of cities date as early as 1500 B.C. Such information as this has vast and important implications on the origin of our Bible, for it was formerly held by skeptical Bible critics that writing was unknown in the days of Moses (*c.* 1500 B.C.) and therefore that Moses could not have been the author of the first five books of the Bible. We now know that writing was generally practiced many centuries before Moses, which means it can no longer be assumed that it was impossible for Moses to have written the books ascribed to him.

Ancient peoples of Palestine and adjoining countries adopted many kinds of materials for writing purposes. The Bible itself makes reference to a number of these materials.

1. Stone. In almost every region the earliest material on which writing has been found is stone. In Egypt and Babylonia the earliest inscriptions are on stone. The oldest considerable portions of Hebrew writing found in Palestine are also on stone. The best examples of these are the famous Moabite Stone and the Siloam Inscription. The Moabite Stone was erected by Mesha, King of Moab, about 850 B.C. and tells of Moab's revolt against Jehoram, King of Israel. The Siloam Inscription records the construction of a tunnel in Jerusalem adjoining the pool of Siloam. The inscription probably comes from the time of King Hezekiah, about 700 B.C. That these early specimens of writing exist on stone is in remarkable agreement with the Bible account, for the earliest writing material mentioned in the Old Testament is stone. The Ten Commandments, as almost everyone knows, were first written on stone. The book of Exodus reads: "And he gave to Moses, when he had made an end of speaking with him upon

Mount Sinai, the two tables of the testimony, tables of stone, written with the finger of God" (Ex. 31:18; *cf.* also Ex. 34:1, 28) . After the people of Israel had crossed the Jordan, they were to set up stones and write the law on them (Deut. 27:2-3; *cf.* Josh. 8:30-32) .

2. Clay. In the countries of Assyria and Babylonia the predominant writing material was clay. Huge libraries of clay tablets have been unearthed from this part of the world. As an example, the library of the Assyrian king Ashurbanipal (*c.* 650 B.C.) has been recovered, containing literally thousands of tablets on all sorts of subjects. In Egypt, also, clay was used. This is evidenced by the discovery of some 350 tablets in the heart of Egypt at a site known as Tell el-Amarna. The tablets, usually oblong in shape, were written on when soft and then were oven-baked or allowed to dry in the sun. This clay material is referred to in Ezekiel 4:1 when the prophet is commanded to sketch a plan of Jerusalem on a tile.

3. Wood. Wooden tablets were used quite generally by the ancients for writing purposes. In Greece wooden tablets provided the common writing surface for many centuries. At Athens in the fourth century B.C., tablets were whitewashed to receive the ink better and were used for official notices. In Egypt and in Palestine wooden writing tablets also were to be found. In Isaiah 30:8 and Habakkuk 2:2 the tablets mentioned are undoubtedly wooden.

4. Leather. For hundreds of years leather or animal skins played an important role in the history of the Bible. Leather is not specified in the Old Testament, but it was unquestionably the principal material employed for literary purposes by the Hebrews. A scribe's knife, used for the purpose of erasures, is mentioned in Jeremiah 36:23. This furnishes good evidence that the scroll mentioned in this verse was a leather scroll, since a sharp instrument like a knife would not have been applied to a delicate writing surface.[1] Other sources of information indicate that

---

[1]This is the view of Sir Frederic Kenyon: *cf.* Kenyon's article entitled "Writing", *A Dictionary of the Bible*, James Hastings, Editor, IV, 945; also Kenyon, *Our Bible and the Ancient Manuscripts*. Revised by A. W. Adams. (New York: Harper & Brothers, 1958), p. 38. A different view associates the scribe's knife with the use of papyrus; *cf. The Interpreter's Bible*, V, 1067.

the Old Testament Scriptures were written on and handed down by means of leather. The Jewish Talmud, a code of traditional laws, required explicitly that the Scriptures be copied on animal skins, which regulation undoubtedly embodies an ancient tradition. It is safe to conclude, therefore, that the Old Testament writings were regularly copied on prepared skins. When in New Testament times the Apostle Paul requests that "the parchments" be sent to him (II Tim. 4:13), it is likely that he is speaking of portions of the Old Testament.

5. Papyrus. The significant role of leather for the Old Testament is played by papyrus in the New. Indeed, papyrus was the most important writing material which could be found in the ancient world and was so widely used that it is practically certain that the original New Testament letters were penned on papyrus sheets. The papyrus plant formerly grew in abundance along the river Nile. This accounts for its early inauguration in Egypt as a writing material, which dates at least as far back as 3500 B.C. The popularity of papyrus spread from Egypt to surrounding countries, and its use was so general that it became the universal medium for the making of books in Greece and Rome. By the time of the fourth century B.C., the use of papyrus was so widespread that the great historian Herodotus could scarcely conceive of civilized people using any other writing material. He writes: "Paper rolls also were called from of old 'parchments' by the Ionians, because formerly when paper was scarce they used, instead, the skins of sheep and goats — on which material many of the barbarians are even now wont to write."[2] By "paper" is meant, of course, not modern paper but papyrus; and Herodotus back in his time called those who did not use papyrus "barbarians."

The production of papyrus sheets is one indication of the skills often achieved by people of the distant past. From the pith of the stem of the papyrus plant thin strips were cut and laid side by side to form a sheet. A second layer was laid across the first and joined to it by moisture and pressure. After drying and polishing the sheet was then ready for use. Sometimes the sheet was used by itself, as for a letter or receipt; at other times several

2Herodotus V. 58.

sheets were joined together to make a roll. Papyrus rolls were the "books" of the ancient world until the first or second century A.D.

Almost everyone has heard of papyrus rolls. What did they look like and how were they used? Papyrus rolls varied in size, but the average roll was about 30 feet long and 9 to 10 inches high. Usually all the writing was done on one side, although at times a scribe might make use of both sides of the roll (cf. Rev. 5:1). The writing was arranged in columns of different widths, the average width being about 3 to 4 inches. Often the inner edge of the roll (sometimes both edges) was attached to a wooden roller to facilitate the rolling and unrolling of the scroll. The title of the work was indicated by placing on the outside of the roll a strip of papyrus with the appropriate designation. Often the roll was put in a protective covering and placed for safe keeping in a wooden case.

About the time of the first or second century A.D., however, the papyrus roll began to give way to what is known as the papyrus *codex.* A codex manuscript is simply what we know today as a book. In other words, not long after the birth of Christ men began to put papyrus sheets together in the form of a book instead of joining them side by side to make a roll. The codex or book-form had distinct advantages over the roll: it could be carried about and used for ready reference, and it could contain more written matter than an average size roll. For these reasons the early Christians, when copying and circulating the New Testament writings, preferred the codex-form instead of the roll-form.

6. Vellum or parchment. Vellum came into prominence as a writing material due to the efforts of King Eumenes II (197-158 B.C.) of Pergamum in Asia Minor. Eumenes was endeavoring to build up his library to world-wide stature, but the king of Egypt moved to stop Eumenes' enterprise by cutting off the supply of papyrus from Egypt. Eumenes' only alternative was to procure his own writing materials, which he did by perfecting an improved process in the treatment of skins. The result of this improvement is known as *vellum* or *parchment.*

Vellum and parchment are now used interchangeably to refer to all kinds of animal skins especially dressed for writing purposes. Originally, however, vellum (related to the English word *veal*) denoted the skins of calves and antelopes, while parchment referred to materials obtained from sheep and goats. Vellum usually suggests a fine quality skin and is distinguished from leather, discussed above, in not being tanned. To learn something about vellum and its place in the history of writing is particularly important because this was the material used for more than a thousand years in making copies of the New Testament. It is in order, therefore, to inquire concerning the preparation of vellum. The difficult process begins when the animal skins are stretched and dried. The hair is removed from one side and the flesh from the other; both sides are then rubbed smooth with stone. Sheets of vellum are cut and folded in the middle to form quires, a process which results in hair-side facing hair-side and flesh-side facing flesh-side. Lines are ruled on the sheets by means of a pointed instrument, which cuts a groove on one side and leaves a ridge on the other. Writing on the vellum codex was done in columns, at first three or four columns to a page and later two to a page.

Vellum manuscripts are beautiful in appearance. The two most valuable New Testament manuscripts in existence today are outstanding representatives of high quality vellum. Sometimes for special effect the vellum was dyed purple and inscribed with gold or silver letters. But the most important feature about vellum is its durability. Papyrus by nature is fragile and subject to decay. For this reason, and because of an eventual shortage of papyrus, it was inevitable that vellum would replace papyrus, and so from the fourth century through the Middle Ages the principal receptacle for the written Word of God was vellum.

7. Paper. Paper also reaches back to the ancient world. Paper production from fibrous matter was practiced by the Chinese people as early as the second century B.C., but it was not until much later before the secret of paper-making became known to the rest of the world. This came about in the middle of the eighth century A.D. when Arabs captured some Chinese prisoners who were skilled in the making of paper. Gradually the knowledge of paper-making spread, and by the time of the thirteenth century paper was being used in much of Europe. A considerable

number of Biblical manuscripts, especially those that originated in the East, are on paper.

8. Other writing materials. Other kinds of materials such as wax, lead, linen, pieces of pottery, etc., were used for writing by the ancients, but the ones mentioned above are those significant in the history of our Bible. Other equipment of the scribe depended on the nature of his writing surface. If the material was clay or wax, a sharp instrument known as a *stylos* was employed. In the case of papyrus a prepared reed was used as the pen. Undoubtedly this is the type of pen mentioned in III John 13. Inks were of different mixtures, but the inks used on vellum manuscripts were of a permanent nature.

Summary

The history of writing leads back to the remote past. Writing was being practiced generally hundreds of years before the time of Moses. It is not a foregone conclusion that Moses could not have written some parts of our Bible. As in our day, people wrote long ago on almost all kinds of materials, depending on their locale and situation in history. For the Old Testament the most important writing material was leather or skins. At the time when the New Testament was penned papyrus was in general use. Shortly afterward the papyrus roll was superceded by the papyrus codex, which was ready-made for Christian purposes. About the fourth century vellum displaced papyrus and so the handmade copies of the New Testament in succeeding centuries took the form of the vellum codex. Thus the vast majority of our New Testament manuscripts stand today written on the handsome and durable material of vellum.

FOR CONSIDERATION

1. What information is available to show that writing was generally practiced before the time of Moses? Of what significance is this information to the authorship of the first five books of the Bible?
2. List some of the main materials used in ancient times for writing. Which of these materials was the most important for the Old Testament Scriptures?

3. Describe the appearance of a papyrus roll. What is the significance of papyrus for the early history of the New Testament?
4. What is meant by a codex? Was it better than the roll? If so, what were some of its advantages?
5. What is vellum? What is the story that lies behind its development? Is it to be distinguished from parchment?
6. How long was vellum used in making copies of the New Testament? Discuss some of the advantages which vellum had over papyrus for the production of New Testaments manuscripts.

2

The Birth of the Bible

It is not possible for us to fix with exact precision the circumstances of the Bible's origin. We cannot go to a specific time and place and say that here the Bible had its birth. As through hundreds of years ancient literary works took shape in many forms, so also from century to century the many books of the Bible were coming into being separately and under varying conditions. The Bible is a collection of books, which indeed is indicated whenever we use the term *Bible*. (The word itself is derived from *biblia*, i.e., the books.) But the Bible is more than an ordinary collection: it is a treasure-house of sacred books which has grown through the centuries until it has attained its present stature. And it is the firm belief of the Christian that the Bible is honored today because in the past it grew under the favorable and directing influence of Him who is the Author of all things.

The Early Form of Our Bible

The Bible has reached its present stature through gradual and almost imperceptible stages of growth. At first and for a long time God's communication to man was oral. In the period known as the Patriarchal Dispensation God spoke directly to such men as Adam, Noah, Abraham and Joseph. But the time came when it was necessary for the divine will to be put in a more permanent form, and that a record of God's revelations be made for succeeding generations. In other words, it was God's purpose that by means of a *written record* He be revealed to all ages and tongues as Creator and Redeemer.

The first person mentioned in the Bible as writing anything is Moses, who lived about 1500 B.C. In the early books of the Bible there are six distinct things attributed to his hand: (1) the memorial concerning Amalek (Ex. 17:14) ; (2) the words of the covenant made at Sinai (Ex. 24:4) ; (3) the Ten Commandments

(Ex. 34:27, 28) ; (4) the journeys of the children of Israel in the wilderness (Num. 33:2) ; (5) the Book of the Law which was to be kept with the Ark of the Covenant (Deut. 31:9, 24) ; (6) the Song found in Deuteronomy 32:1-43 (Deut. 31:22). In addition, Moses is held by strict Jewish tradition as being the author of the first five books of the Bible known as the Pentateuch. Other writers of the Bible, and the Lord himself, gave unvarying support to this view (*cf.* Josh. 8:31; Judg. 3:4; Mal. 4:4; Luke 24:44; John 7:19).

When once divine revelation was put in writing, it was natural for other revelations and events to be recorded. So the successor of Moses, Joshua, also wrote words "in the book of the law of God" (Josh. 24:26). This in turn became the practice of other men of God who wrote both history and prophecy. In the book of I Samuel it is said that the venerable Samuel recorded certain events of his day in a book. We read: "Then Samuel told the people the rights and duties of the kingship; and he wrote them in a book and laid it up before the Lord" (I Sam. 10:25). Prophets in later times also are engaged in writing books. God speaks to Jeremiah and says: "Take a scroll and write on it all the words that I have spoken to you against Israel and Judah and all the nations, from the day I spoke to you, from the days of Josiah until today" (Jer. 36:2). The result is that later generations are found consulting the writings of their esteemed predecessors. Daniel searches "in the books" and finds that the prophet Jeremiah limited the duration in which Jerusalem was to be ravaged by the enemy to seventy years (Dan. 9:2). And when later the people are assembled in the newly rebuilt Jerusalem, it is the law of Moses that is read and honored (Neh. 8:1-8). So the books of Moses' law came first, then came the prophets. In this way the Old Testament Scriptures grew gradually and finally came to be assembled into an accepted collection about the time of Ezra (*c.* 400 B.C.). The Jewish authority, Josephus, writing in the time of the first century, said that no book was added to the Hebrew Scriptures after the time of Malachi.[1]

---

[1]Josephus, *Against Apion* I. 8. Actually, Josephus marks off the interval of the Old Testament canon as being from Moses to the Persian king Artaxerxes. The time of Artaxerxes was the time of Ezra, Nehemiah and Malachi.

The New Testament came into being gradually also, although the books themselves were written in a comparatively short period of time (50-100 A.D.). These books were simply letters penned by inspired men and addressed to different churches and individuals. From the first, however, they were looked upon as distinctively authoritative writings; and thus they were received with respect and read in the public assemblies wherever Christians worshipped (I Thess. 5:27). Soon afterward came the interchange of extant letters among the churches (*cf.* Col. 4:16), the individual churches in this way profiting from an exchange of apostolic instructions. The next step was the embodiment in writing of the central events of the life of Jesus. At first oral accounts of his work by eyewitnesses filled the needs of the infant church, but as years passed eyewitness accounts became few and insufficient. Now the demand was for authoritative written narratives, and in fulfillment of this demand Matthew, Mark, Luke and John sent out their witness to Jesus (*cf.* Luke 1:1-4; John 20:30-31). The logical outgrowth of the Four Gospels was the book of Acts which told the story of the primitive church; and as a kind of climax to the whole came Revelation with its prospect of a triumphant Christ. The result of it all was that a new community of people, just like the people of the Old Covenant, had as a cherished treasure their own writings as "Scripture."

The Form of Our Bible Today

Our Bible today, as everyone knows, is divided into two major sections known as the Old and New Testaments. The term *testament* is an unfortunate translation (Greek, *diatheke*) and would be better rendered as *contract or covenant*. Thus the basic structure of the Bible hinges on the idea that God has made two significant covenants with his people, and that the New Covenant has displaced the Old. The Old Covenant appears in our English Bibles in the following arrangement: (1) five books of Law or the Pentateuch (Genesis to Deuteronomy); (2) twelve books of History (Joshua to Esther); (3) five books of Poetry (Job to Song of Solomon); and (4) seventeen books of Prophecy (Isaiah to Malachi), sometimes subdivided into five books of Major Prophets and twelve books of Minor Prophets. This arrangement of Old Testament books found in English Bibles is derived

from the Latin Vulgate translation, which in turn is derived
from the Septuagint or Greek version.

The books of the Hebrew Bible, however, are grouped differently. As one picks up a copy of it he sees the following
order:

1. Law: Genesis, Exodus, Leviticus, Numbers, Deuteronomy.
2. Prophets:
   a. Former Prophets: Joshua, Judges, I and II Samuel, I and
      II Kings.
   b. Latter Prophets: Isaiah, Jeremiah, Ezekiel and the Book
      of the Twelve.
3. Writings: Psalms, Proverbs, Job, Song of Solomon, Ruth,
   Lamentations, Ecclesiastes, Esther, Daniel, Ezra-Nehemiah,
   I and II Chronicles.

If we compare this arrangement with our English Bible we see
that the Hebrew Bible has but three major divisions: the Law,
the Prophets, and the Writings (*cf.* Luke 24:44). There is not
only a different structure, but also different designations for the
books. The twelve Minor Prophets, for example, are taken together as one book and are known simply as the Twelve. Another
prominent difference appears by terming Joshua, Judges, and the
books of Samuel and Kings as Former Prophets. These books
which we regard as historical are known as prophetic because
they were written with a prophetic outlook by men who most
likely were prophets. However different the arrangement, it is
important to remember that the books included in the English
Bible are precisely the same as found in the Hebrew Bible.

The books of the New Covenant are grouped together in
three parts: (1) five books of History (Matthew to Acts), twenty-
one books of Doctrine (Romans to Jude), and one book of
prophecy (Revelation).

(1) The five books of History may be further divided into
the Four Gospels and Acts of the Apostles. The Gospels are so
called because they present the message of God's good news revealed in Jesus Christ. In a larger sense they may be referred to as
lives of Jesus, but in the strict sense they are not biographies but
mere sketches of some of the great achievements of that unique
Life. The first three Gospels are known as the Synoptic Gospels
because of their similar contents. The Gospel of John was writ-

ten at a later date and presupposes the presence and knowledge of the first three narratives. The Acts of the Apostles is a kind of continuation of the Gospel of Luke, and since both works were from the hand of Luke, and because of their interconnection, they are sometimes referred to as Luke-Acts.

(2) The twenty-one books of Doctrine are epistles written by various inspired men. The first thirteen in this group bear the name of Paul. The Pauline Epistles are of two groups: those written before his two years' imprisonment in Rome (*cf.* Acts 28:30) ; and those written later (I and II Timothy and Titus) which are sometimes called the Pastoral Epistles. The book of Hebrews is sometimes numbered in the Pauline group, although its authorship remains a question mark.

The General or Catholic (universal) Epistles are comprised of James, the letters of Peter and John, and Jude. In the early Greek manuscripts these books are found immediately following the Acts of the Apostles and before the Pauline collection of letters.

(3) The one book of Prophecy, the book of Revelation or Apocalypse, perhaps was not the last book of the New Testament to be written, but it suitably appears at the end of the Bible since it summarizes in symbolic language the principles revealed in preceding books and at the same times gives a prophetic foretaste of things to come.

The Languages of the Bible

It has been seen that the Bible has come to be what it is today through gradual stages of growth. It remains now for us to give some attention to the languages in which the various books of the Bible were originally composed. Our English translations are beautiful literary works in themselves; but it will aid the Bible student immeasurably to know something of the Bible languages, and a knowledge about these languages will fill in for him another link in the history of the Bible.

The Bible was written originally in three languages: (1) Hebrew, (2) Aramaic, and (3) Greek. Contrary to the opinion of some people, these languages are not dead languages. Hebrew is the spoken language of the new state of Israel; Aramaic is spoken by a few Christians in the environs of Syria; and Greek, of course, is spoken by millions of people today, although it is quite different from the Greek of the New Testament.

(1) Hebrew. Almost all of the thirty-nine books of the Old Testament are written in Hebrew. Hebrew is of a large family of languages known as *Semitic*, and is akin to such languages as Aramaic, Syriac, Akkadian (Assyrian-Babylonian) and Arabic. To people of the Western hemisphere Hebrew is a "strange" language. It is written "backwards" (from right to left), has many sounds that are foreign to ears accustomed to English forms, and possesses a vocabulary that is unrelated to English words. The forms of the Hebrew alphabet likewise present a problem and sometimes are confused by the best-trained eye. (The King James and American Standard reader can turn to Psalms 119, the sections of which are numbered according to the Hebrew letters, and get a sample of the Hebrew alphabet.) In addition, the Hebrew alphabet is without vowels. It is true that a system of vowel-points has been added which gives untold aid in the study of the language, but to a person thoroughly trained in the language this vowel system often proves a hindrance as much as a help. Modern Hebrew books and magazines are normally printed without vowels; and this is precisely the way the Old Testament text originally appeared.

(2) Aramaic. Aramaic is a kindred language to Hebrew, and after the time of the exile (*c.* 500 B.C.) became the tongue of the common man in Palestine. (Nehemiah 8:8 is usually taken in the sense that the people did not know pure Hebrew and therefore needed a translation into the familiar Aramaic.) Since Aramaic was spoken by the Jews several centuries before Christ, it is not surprising to find some portions of the Old Testament in Aramaic instead of Hebrew. Aramaic sections of the Old Testament include: one word as a place-name in Genesis 31:47; one verse in Jeremiah 10:11; about six chapters in the book of Daniel (2:4b — 7:28); and several chapters in Ezra (4:8 — 6:18; 7:12-26). To anyone who looks at a copy of the Hebrew Bible these sections will appear no different from other parts of the Old Testament. This is true because the Aramaic characters are like those of the Hebrew, or to be more exact, the square-shaped Hebrew letters are actually borrowed from the Aramaic. So there

is no difference in appearance between Hebrew and Aramaic, but the two are distinct languages.

The longest Old Testament section in Aramaic begins in Daniel 2:4. The first part of this verse is in Hebrew, and the Aramaic portion starts with the response of the Chaldeans, "O king, live forever!" An interesting confirmation of this linguistic change within the verse has come to light in the last few years. The amazing Dead Sea Scrolls have produced a little fragment of this section of Daniel and in the middle of Daniel 2:4 the Hebrew stops and the Aramaic begins — exactly as our text reads two thousand years later.

Aramaic continued for centuries as the vernacular of Palestine. The New Testament preserves for us Aramaic expressions of Jesus, such as *talitha cumi* (little girl, get up) in Mark 5:41; *ephphatha* (be opened) in Mark 7:34; *Eli eli, lama sabachthani* (My God, my God, why hast thou forsaken me?) in Matthew 27:46. Jesus habitually addressed God as *Abba* (Aramaic for Father), which did not fail to leave its mark on the vocabulary of the early church (Rom. 8:15; Gal. 4:6). Another common Aramaic phrase of early Christians was *Marana tha,* which means "Our Lord, come!" (I Cor. 16:22). These expressions clearly show that the language normally spoken by our Lord and his Jewish followers was Aramaic.

(3) Greek. Although the spoken language of Jesus was Aramaic, the books which comprise our New Testament were written in Greek. There is little question today on this point, although a few men have maintained that some portions of the New Testament were issued at first in Aramaic. It was in the providence of God, since the gospel was to be proclaimed to every creature, that the New Testament writers made use of a language that was known everywhere. Greek in the first century, as English is today, was the "universal" language.

The Greek of the New Testament exhibits certain linguistic peculiarities. For a long time it was affirmed that these peculiarities could be explained on no other basis than the supposition of a "Holy Ghost Greek." Recent discoveries and research have wholly overthrown this supposition, and now the language of the New Testament is more correctly termed Hellenistic or *Koine* (common) Greek. We have been brought to this unmistakable conclusion due largely to discoveries among the Greek papyri. The significance of these papyri finds can scarcely be over-exaggerated. Their impact on the Greek text and its vocabulary will be considered later.

Summary

Our Bible is a collection of extraordinary books written over a period of sixteen hundred years. The Bible gradually grew until its completion near the close of the first century A.D. As a collection of books the Bible through the years has been arranged in various ways. The order of books in our English Old Testament goes back to the Greek version which was used widely in the early church. Our New Testament writings are arranged according to a logical pattern, although different orders can be found among various manuscripts. The languages of the Bible are three in number: Hebrew, Aramaic and Greek. Some of the Old Testament was written in Aramaic, but Hebrew was the predominant language. By the time of the first century Greek had become a world-wide language, which accounts for the New Testament being written in Greek.

For Consideration

1. Who is mentioned in the Bible as being the first author of anything? What evidence is available to show that he is the author of the Pentateuch?

2. At about what time were the books of the New Testament written? How does this compare to the interval of time during which the Old Testament books originated?

3. Describe the arrangement of Old Testament books in the English Bible. How does this compare to the Hebrew arrangement? Are the books the same in each?

4. What are the three main divisions of the New Testament? Which writer is responsible for the largest group of New Testament books?

5. What are the Synoptic Gospels, and in what group do they belong? What are the Catholic epistles? What arrangement do they often have in some of the early manuscripts? What is the Apocalypse?

6. Name the three original languages in which the Bible was written. Is it correct to speak of them as "dead languages"?

7. In what language were the books of the New Testament written? Was this the native language of Jesus? If not, what was the language normally spoken by Jesus? How do we know this?

Manuscripts of the New Testament

We have seen that the New Testament letters made their appearance in the latter half of the first century. We have noted also that these letters were written undoubtedly on papyrus sheets. Papyrus was used widely, but had the disadvantage of being a fragile writing material. So very soon after the New Testament letters were penned the original autographs perished. Yet God's word was not hopelessly lost. The different New Testament letters had been received with the authority of heaven behind them, which prompted early Christians to make many copies of these precious apostolic messages. These copies of the New Testament in Greek are known simply as *manuscripts*. (The word *manuscript* basically denotes anything written by hand, but by general consent in connection with the Bible it is restricted to the documents of the original tongues. Thus a New Testament manuscript is a *Greek* manuscript.)

Let us suppose that we have a New Testament manuscript before our eyes. The first thing to learn about it is its age. How old is it? What means do we use in dating it? In answering these questions we must look carefully at the handwriting. Are the letters large or small? Are the words all written together, or are there spaces between the words? How many columns are there to a page, and what is the length of the columns? Are there any marks of punctuation or divisions into paragraphs? What is the form of the letters? Are they plain and simple or elaborate and complex? These are some of the basic points to look for when one examines a manuscript. Actually, a trained specialist will observe many other things, and through technical knowledge and experience can come to an accurate determination of the date of any given manuscript.

New Testament manuscripts are of two major types, the form of the letters supplying the key in determining those types. The manuscripts of one group, the earliest and certainly the most important one, are written in capital letters and are known as *uncials*. The handwriting found in a larger group is smaller and in a running hand-style, so these manuscripts are known as *cursives*. The cursives did not make their debut until the ninth century and thus are of less value because of their late dates.

The number of our New Testament manuscripts is vast, about 4,500 in all. All of these, however, are not complete New Testaments. In fact, only a few contain anything like what could be termed a complete New Testament. Yet the New Testament is without a doubt the best-attested book from the ancient world. Most of the manuscripts do not contain the entire New Testament for the simple reason that a hand-produced copy of the whole was too bulky for practical use. Our present manuscripts indicate that four categories were generally followed when making copies of the New Testament: (1) the Four Gospels, (2) the Acts and General Epistles, (3) the Pauline Epistles, and (4) the book of Revelation. Often groups (2), (3), and (4) were combined into one to form a second volume, with the Four Gospels naturally serving as volume one. In other words, the New Testament was often broken down into separate volumes and this is why most of our manuscripts today do not contain all of the twenty-seven books. Of the known 4,500 manuscripts, the vast majority are cursives which date from the ninth to the fifteenth century, while those of uncial script number altogether about 300.

When the New Testament was first written the literary style was of uncial character. This means that the letters of the apostles were inscribed in large letters, without intervening spaces between the words, and with no marks of punctuation. How Paul's letter to the Romans appeared to his readers may be illustrated as follows:

PAULASERVANTOFJESUSCHRISTCALLEDTOBE
ANAPOSTLESEPARATEDUNTOTHEGOSPELOFG
ODWHICHHEPROMISEDAFORETHROUGHTHEP

This looks something like Paul's original letter, except that Paul

A Fragment of the Gospel of John. This is the oldest known manuscript of any part of the New Testament. It contains John 18:31-33, 37, 38, and is dated in the first half of the second century. Courtesy of the John Rylands Library.

may have used abbreviations for familiar words and, of course, wrote in Greek instead of English. Notice also that an unfinished word was completed on the line below in order to keep the columns straight.

The uncial hand, as mentioned above, is represented today in about 300 manuscripts. This number includes about seventy papyri documents, dating from the second to the fourth century. Broken pieces of pottery known as *ostraca* were sometimes used for writing, of which about thirty fragments have come down to us with portions of the New Testament written on them. Such finds as the papyri and ostraca have taken place mostly within the last seventy-five years, and contribute a great deal to our knowledge of the New Testament text. Excluding the papyri and ostraca, this means that there are extant about 200 uncial manuscripts copied on vellum, and these date from the fourth to the ninth century.

The Important Uncials

By and large the most important copies of the Scriptures are the oldest ones. Fortunately, our oldest vellum manuscripts are complete or almost complete copies of the New Testament. These old copies are three in number and are known as the Vatican, the Sinaitic, and the Alexandrian manuscripts. They date back to A.D. 300-450. Aged, worn, faded, and unattractive in many respects, these are the greatest document-treasures in Christendom — the oldest Bibles in the world!

1. The Vatican Manuscript. This fourth century manuscript is acknowledged widely as being the most important witness on the text of the New Testament. As its name implies, it is located in the Vatican Library at Rome. It has resided here at least since 1481, the date of a catalog in which it is listed. As Sir Frederic Kenyon has remarked, there is no story to tell of the manuscript's discovery; the interesting story that attaches to the manuscript relates to the continued efforts of many scholars over the years to publish its contents for the world. Not until the close of the last century did the exact contents of the manuscript become available. Kenyon describes the long struggle which led up to that time: "A correspondent of Erasmus in 1533 sent that scholar a number of selected readings from it, as proof of its superiority

to the received Greek text. In 1669 a collation (or statement of its various readings) was made by Bartolocci, but it was never published, and remained unknown until 1819. Other imperfect collations were made about 1720 and 1780. Napoleon carried the manuscript off as a prize of victory to Paris, where it remained till 1815, when the many treasures of which he had despoiled the libraries of the Continent were returned to their respective owners. While at Paris it was studied by Hug, and its great age and supreme importance were first fully known; but after its return to Rome a period of seclusion set in. In 1843 Tischendorf, after waiting for several months, was allowed to see it for six hours. Next year De Muralt was permitted to study it for nine hours. In 1845 the great English scholar Tregelles was allowed indeed to see it but not to copy a word. His pockets were searched before he might open it, and all writing materials were taken away. Two clerics stood beside him and snatched away the volume if he looked too long at any passage! However, the Roman authorities now took the task in hand themselves, and in 1857 and 1859 editions by Cardinal Mai were published, which however, differed so much from one another and were both so inaccurate as to be almost useless. In 1866 Tischendorf once more applied for permission to edit the MS., but with difficulty obtained leave to examine it for the purpose of collating difficult passages. Unfortunately the great scholar so far forgot himself as to copy out twenty pages in full, contrary to the conditions under which he had been allowed access to the MS., and his permission was naturally withdrawn. Renewed entreaty procured him six days' longer study, making in all fourteen days of three hours each; and by making the very most of his time Tischendorf was able in 1867 to publish the most perfect edition of the manuscript which had yet appeared. An improved Roman edition appeared in 1868-81; but the final and decisive publication was reserved for the years 1889-90, when a complete photographic facsimile of the whole MS. made its contents once and for all the common property of all scholars."[1]

The Vatican Manuscript (abbreviated as Codex B) is a rare gem in that it contains in Greek practically all of the Old and

[1]Sir Frederic Kenyon, *Our Bible and the Ancient Manuscripts*. Revised by A. W. Adams. (New York: Harper & Brothers, 1958), pp. 202-203.

New Testaments. The beginning has been lost, as far as Genesis 46:28; some of the Psalms are also missing (Psalms 106-138) ; and the ending likewise has dropped off (Hebrews 9:14 to the close, the letters of Timothy and Titus, and Revelation.) The General Epistles are included after the book of Acts, following the usual order of the early uncials. It is bound in book form (a codex) and embraces 759 leaves of the finest vellum. Each page is about ten inches square and holds three columns of writing which originally were very handsome. The beauty of the handwriting has been marred by some later scribe who thought he could do future generations a great service by tracing over the text whose ink was beginning to fade. The scribe actually would have performed a greater service if he had left the manuscript alone, for even after 1600 years the original ink has not faded from view.

It is distressing that the Vatican Manuscript is not entirely complete, yet in spite of its gaps it is considered to be the most exact copy of the New Testament known. It is believed to be the earliest of the great uncials, and the many extensive studies which have proved its text of the purest quality confirm this judgment. The printed texts of the Greek New Testament today rely heavily on the Vatican Codex.

One other point worthy of note concerns the ending of the Gospel of Mark. A fuller discussion of this difficult problem will appear later, but it is sufficient now to observe that the Vatican Manuscript does not include Mark 16:9-20. For some strange reason, however, its scribe left at this point more than a column of space blank in his manuscript. This seems to indicate that he knew of the existence of these questioned verses, but was undecided as to whether he should include them or not.

(2) The Sinaitic Manuscript. Of almost equal importance to the Vatican Manuscript is the Sinaitic Codex. It is known as the Sinaitic Manuscript because it was "discovered" by the great text-critic Constantine Tischendorf at St. Catharine's Monastery on Mt. Sinai. This manuscript goes by the abbreviation of Codex Aleph. (Aleph is the first letter in the Hebrew alphabet.)

No story is more fascinating than that of the discovery of the Sinaitic Codex. In 1844 Tischendorf, while visiting the Monastery, stumbled on a basket full of old parchments which were destined for the fire. On examination he found numerous sheets of the Greek version of the Old Testament. Tischendorf had worked with many manuscripts, but these leaves were clearly the oldest he had ever seen. He was permitted to take away with him a number of these old sheets, but he could not keep to himself the thrill of his discovery. His exuberance over his find so aroused the suspicion of the monastery that its authorities would not co-operate with him further. The next fifteen years were to mark attempt after attempt by Tischendorf to gain other manuscripts, but all in vain.

By the year of 1859 Tischendorf, still in quest of the wonderful documents, had formed a friendship with the Emperor of Russia; and since St. Catharine's was a Greek Orthodox Monastery, the patronage of the Russian ruler would prove to be very valuable. So with the backing of the Russian Czar, Tischendorf again came to Mt. Sinai. Day after day his most careful searches turned up nothing. On the night before his scheduled departure the next morning, the steward of the monastery happened to mention to him that he had an old copy of the Scriptures. By this time Tischendorf had given up and could see in his mind these old manuscripts being used as fuel for some monk's fire. One can imagine his utter amazement when, after fifteen years of anxiety and on the last night of his visit, the manuscripts shown to him by the steward were the very ones he had been looking for. Not only did he have in front of him part of the Old Testament, but the entire New Testament as well, with all twenty-seven books complete. But this time the renowned scholar was self-composed and almost indifferently asked if he might take the steward's copy to his room. Only when back in the privacy of his quarters did he let his emotions go. Then through the rest of the night he worked with his priceless Biblical treasures, for, as he later explained, "that night it seemed sacrilege to sleep." Eventually, and after a long train of events, Tischendorf succeeded in obtaining the manuscript as a gift to the Russian Czar. But Russia was not to be its permanent home. In 1933 the Soviet Authorities, more interested in money than Bibles, sold the Sinaitic Codex to the British for the sum of 100,000 pounds, and since that time Tischendorf's greatest find has reposed in the manuscript room of the British Museum.

The Sinaitic Manuscript. This page shows the close of Mark's Gospel and the beginning of the Gospel of Luke. In this manuscript the Gospel of Mark concludes with verse 8.

At one time the Sinaitic Manuscript evidently contained the complete Old Testament, but much of it had been lost before its discovery by Tischendorf. Fortunately, the New Testament portion is intact, and includes also two other non-canonical books known as the Epistle of Barnabas and the Shepherd of Hermas. These two early Christian works, which for a while remained on the border line of the canon, will be discussed later. The leaves in the Sinaitic Manuscript are larger than those of the Vatican Codex and measure approximately fifteen inches square. The handwriting is large and clear, and is imposed four columns to the page on vellum of outstanding quality. Tischendorf's first impression as to its antiquity has proved true, and it is generally conceded that it should be dated from the middle of the fourth century. Its early date, of course, makes it highly valuable. Extensive textual studies have classed it in type with the Vatican Manuscript, all of which means that the two most important witnesses for the Greek New Testament are the Vatican and Sinaitic Codices.

3. The Alexandrian Manuscript. Brief mention needs to be made of a fifth-century uncial, the Alexandrian Codex. Its name is derived from Alexandria, the place from which it originally came. It was offered by Cyril Lucar, a high official of the Greek church, as a gift to James I of England. But James died before the gift could be completed, and so in 1627 it was presented to his successor Charles I. Since that time it has passed down through the royal families and has taken up residence in the British Museum.

The Alexandrian Codex (Codex A) is of both testaments, but is defective at points. Only ten leaves are missing from the Old Testament, but twenty-five leaves have dropped off from the beginning of Matthew, two leaves from John, and three from II Corinthians. As to the quality of its contents, it does not quite measure up to the high standard set by the Vatican and Sinaitic Manuscripts.

When the Alexandrian Codex was first presented to the English king it caused as much excitement at that time as the discovery of the Dead Sea Scrolls has in our day. It was the first of the three great uncials to come to light, and its different readings from current translations were to usher in a new era of textual investigation.

Many other noteworthy uncials could be considered, but two in particular will be discussed in the next chapter. Each of the 4,500 manuscripts in existence today has its own story, and even though numbers of them are relatively unimportant as compared with the great uncials yet each stands as an independent witness to our New Testament.

Summary

Manuscripts of the Greek New Testament fall into two major divisions: uncials and cursives. The uncials are those penned in large, capital letters, while the cursives are those which are written similar to our longhand script. Most of our manuscripts are cursives, since they are dated from the ninth century on. The vellum uncials, some of which date back from the fourth century, are of inestimable worth as witnesses to the New Testament books. The "big three" of the uncials, listed in accord with their importance, are the Vatican, the Sinaitic, and Alexandrian Manuscripts. Two of these have become accessible within the last century, and all three have become known since the translation of the King James Bible.

For Consideration

1. What is a manuscript? Discuss some of the ways the dates of manuscripts can be determined.
2. Distinguish between *uncials* and *cursives*. Which is the most important group as evidence on the New Testament text? Why?
3. Give the names of the three oldest and most valuable copies of the New Testament. Where is each manuscript located today?
4. Describe briefly some of the main features of the Vatican Codex. How does it rank in importance?
5. Who was Constantine Tischendorf? What part did he play in the "discovery" of the Sinaitic Manuscript?
6. Were any of the three great uncials available at the time of the King James translation?

4

Other Manuscripts and
New Testament Witnesses

Nothing is more thrilling than for one to look with his own eyes and to hold in his own hands some manuscript of the New Testament. The many New Testament manuscripts are scattered all over the world. In America most of the large university libraries, especially in the Eastern section of the country, house some of these Biblical treasures. You may go to such centers of learning as Harvard, Princeton, Duke, and Chicago, ask the curator for the privilege of seeing some manuscripts, and there gain a first-hand acquaintance with the materials which have preserved for us our Bible.

We have learned that the most important manuscripts are those of the uncial group. The three main uncials, the Vatican, the Sinaitic, and the Alexandrian, provide in the main the foundation for our New Testament books. This is not to leave the impression that all other manuscripts and witnesses are of little value. Indeed, without the many other textual authorities we could not evaluate properly these three great uncials. Attention is now turned to other data which cast welcomed light on the New Testament.

We have seen that the Alexandrian Manuscript dates back to the fifth century. Also from the fifth century come two other key manuscripts which should be mentioned.

(4) The Manuscript of Ephraem. At different times materials used in writing have become difficult to obtain. This was often the case in the Middle Ages. One way to overcome this shortage was to take an old parchment, wash or scrape off the ink, and then write over the old handwriting. This kind of manuscript is

known technically as a *palimpsest,* a Greek term which has passed into English and literally means *rubbed again.* Not a few old parchments like this have come down to us, some having been used several times.

The Codex of Ephraem (Codex C) is a palimpsest (or rescript) manuscript. In other words, it has two layers of writing on it. The top layer of writing is a twelfth-century copy of the works of Ephraem of Syria, which explains why it is known as the Codex of Ephraem. But the earlier writing underneath is much more important, for it is a fifth-century copy of the Scriptures. Much is missing from the Old Testament, but for the New Testament there are 145 leaves from every book except II Thessalonians and II John. It was not until 1845 that a full edition of this manuscript was published. The Ephraem Codex is now preserved in the National Library of Paris and its great age alone is sufficient to rank it as an extremely valuable witness for the New Testament.

(5) The Codex Bezae (Codex D). In 1581 Theodore Beza presented this manuscript to the University of Cambridge, where it has remained since. It is the earliest known Biblical copy in two languages, Greek and Latin. The Greek and Latin texts face each other, the Greek on the left side and the Latin on the right. Because its leaves are small (10 by 8 inches), only one column appears to the page. It contains only the Gospels and Acts, with a few verses from the General Epistles.

Codex Bezae has the dubious distinction of being the most curious of all the early manuscripts. Its additions and omissions at times put it in a class by itself. Beza himself looked with suspicion upon his manuscript, as did many of his contemporaries. At the time the King James Version was made Codex Bezae was the only important uncial available, but it was little used because of the speculation that surrounded it. Only in more recent years has it attained, in spite of its pecularities, its deserved attention as an important New Testament authority.

The Cursives

The *cursives,* those written in a running hand, form by far the larger group of our manuscripts. More than 2,500 cursives have now been cataloged, but their dates (from the ninth to the fifteenth century) naturally tend to limit their value. Nevertheless the cursives are witnesses, and some of them contribute much toward our New Testament text. Take for an example a manuscript which is commonly known as "the Queen of the Cursives" (Codex 33). Although this is a ninth-century manuscript, it is very similar in text-type to the great Vatican Codex and therefore as a cursive is more important than many uncials.

Perhaps the greatest item of interest about the cursives is their appearance. Many of these manuscripts are awesome to look at due to their elaborate, artistic decorations. When one goes to a cursive codex, he will often find the covers richly stamped, headings and initial letters luxuriously ornamented, and multi-colored illustrations included with the text. Of most frequent occurrence are the portraits of the authors of the Four Gospels. These arts were popularly practiced in the latter half of the Middle Ages, and almost invariably exhibit the manuscripts in which they are found as being of late origin.

The Lectionaries

One further word needs to be added in order to make the story of New Testament manuscripts complete. Included in the number of our New Testament manuscripts is a group of materials known as *lectionaries*. The term *lection* refers to a selected passage of Scripture designed to be read in the public worship services, and thus a lectionary is a manuscript especially arranged in sections for this purpose. Most lectionaries are of the Gospels, but some are of Acts and the Epistles. Lectionaries cannot be classified as uncials or cursives because there are extant copies of both types. Studies have shown that lectionaries, being designed especially for public worship, were copied a little more carefully than ordinary manuscripts; this means that an eleventh-century lectionary on an average will prove as valuable as a tenth-century codex. More than 1,800 lectionaries have now been enumerated.

The Versions

We have now finished a survey of the primary sources for the New Testament text. We come now to consider materials that, in comparison with the manuscripts, are of a secondary rank,

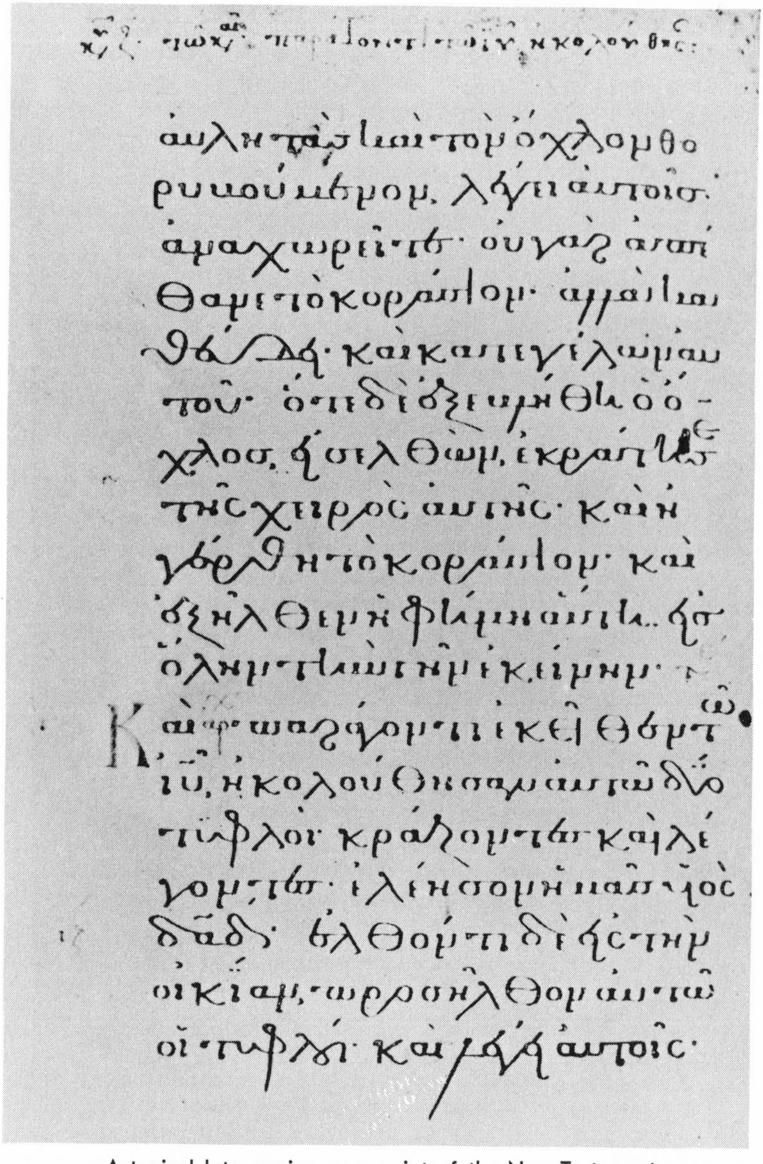

A typical late cursive manuscript of the New Testament

yet are valuable witnesses in their own right. Principal among these is the witness of the *versions* or translations. The gospel that needed proclamation in different tongues on the day of Pentecost was the same gospel, when written, which demanded translation into other languages. After the apostolic messages began to circulate in Greek among early Christians, the next step was to circulate these same messages in other tongues. Wherever Greek was unknown or unnatural, translations from Greek into the native languages began to spring up. A number of these translations were made very shortly after the New Testament books were first issued, and for this reason they offer a wealth of knowledge on the New Testament text.

(1) The Syriac Versions. Syriac was the chief language spoken in the regions of Syria and Mesopotamia and is almost identical to Aramaic. It was undoubtedly one of the earliest translations to be made; for it could be used not only by the Jews who did not know Greek but also by the natives of Mesopotamia, where it is known as a matter of historical record that the gospel had entered before the close of the first century.

(a) The Old Syriac. Only in about the last hundred years has it become known that there was such an early translation of the Bible as the Old Syriac. There are two chief manuscripts of the Old Syriac: the Curetonian Syriac and the Sinaitic Syriac. The Curetonian Syriac is a fifth-century copy of the Gospels, consisting of eighty leaves. It is so called because of the labors of Dr. Cureton of the British Museum. In 1848 he demonstrated that the text of this manuscript is of an earlier type than that of the common Syriac.

The other important witness of the Old Syriac is the Sinaitic Syriac, a manuscript discovered as recently as 1892 at St. Catherine's Monastery on Mt. Sinai. This is a rescript manuscript of the Gospels, of which about one-fourth is not decipherable. It is considered to be a little earlier than the Curetonian Syriac and is the most important Old Syriac document. These two Old Syriac witnesses are of real value because they were copied from a text which evidently goes back to the second century, within a generation or two from the close of the apostolic age.

(b) The Peshitta. The word *Peshitta* means *simple* or *common* and refers to the standard Syriac translation which has been in use since the fifth century. There are about 250 manuscripts of the Peshitta, but the testimony of these manuscripts is not as fundamental as that of the Old Syriac.

(2) The Latin Versions. These versions should hold special interest for all English-speaking people because the first translation of the English Bible was made from the Latin. This was the case because the Latin Bible was for many centuries the Bible for Great Britain and all of Western Europe.

(a) The Old Latin. The Old Latin version, like the Old Syriac, goes back to a very early date. It undoubtedly originated sometime in the second century, probably about A.D. 150. Unlike the Old Syriac, it is represented by a number of copies, about twenty, not including fragments. Some of these Old Latin copies are as old as the celebrated Vatican and Sinaitic Manuscripts. The Old Latin is by far the most important of the Latin versions since it reaches back very close to the time when the last books of the New Testament were written.

(b) The Latin Vulgate. By the time of the fourth century the Old Latin version had been widely copied and circulated in the West. But all of the copies had not been carefully made, and it was obvious that something had to be done in order to keep the Western Bible free from corruption. Somehow a revision had to be made which thereafter would be recognized as an authoritative standard for the Latin-speaking churches. In 382 Damasus, bishop of Rome, was able to gain the services of Jerome for this undertaking. Fortunately, Jerome was eminently qualified for the job, combining the rare qualities of education, consecration and common sense. He began his revision reluctantly, realizing that many would object if he attempted to correct the current version, even if the correction was in agreement with earlier textual authorities. In 384 Jerome finished his work on the Gospels, and later (date unknown) completed the rest of the New Testament. As expected his labors were not at first well received, especially by those people who, according to Jerome, identified "ignorance with holiness." Yet his work was not as revolutionary as he himself would have liked it to be. What Jerome accomplished, then, was a revision of a certain form of the Old Latin version — a revision of a version and not an independent translation.

Within a few years, however, Jerome's edition of the Latin Bible had become the standard authority that Damasus had sought to create. What followed amounted to a thousand years' reign of the Vulgate in the West. While in the East devoted scribes were toiling carefully to transmit the Word of God in Greek, Western scribes were seeking just as conscientiously to preserve the Word of God in Latin. The feverish activity on the part of the Western scribe, together with the advance of Roman Christianity, accounts for the fact that there are extant more copies of the New Testament in the Latin Vulgate (perhaps 10,000) than of the original Greek tongue.

Thus it is scarcely possible to over-estimate the influence of Jerome on our Bible. For more than a thousand years every translation of the Scriptures in Western Europe was based on Jerome's Vulgate. Even after men rightfully turned back to the Greek instead of the Latin for the basis of their translations, still the Vulgate continued to assert its influence. Even in the King James Version the Latin Vulgate is reflected to a greater degree than most people suspect.

Eventually Jerome's Vulgate was made the official Bible of the Roman Catholic Church, and so it remains today. The Roman Catholic Bible in English is actually a translation of a translation, and is not as the Protestant Bible a translation from the original Greek language.

(3) Other versions. Numerous other versions — the Egyptian versions, the Armenian, the Gothic, the Ethiopic, and the Arabic — made their appearance in the early centuries of the Christian era. Some of these translations also were in general use before our earliest vellum uncials were prepared. A knowledge of these versions is the result of recent investigations. Indeed, new materials affecting them are still coming in, and further studies are yet to be made. We cannot expect from these versions any light that will materially alter our text, but we do anticipate information that will provide additional independent testimony to the reliability of our early uncial text.

The Fathers

Another great blessing for the history of the Bible is a large body of literature written by the early Christian Fathers. These

Christian writers lived near the end of the first century, and shortly afterward. The most important of these for the New Testament text include Justin Martyr, Tatian, Irenaeus, and Clement of Alexandria, all of the second century; Origen, Tertullian and Cyprian, of the third century; and in the fourth century the famous names of Eusebius of Caesarea and Jerome. Volume after volume of their writings have been preserved, many of which are literally filled with quotations of the New Testament Scriptures. These men lived long ago and possessed copies of the Scriptures which are naturally older than our manuscripts today. How their many quotations read certainly tells us much concerning the ancient Bible of the primitive church.

Summary

In this chapter two other manuscripts have been added to the list of the important uncials. Altogether this makes five vellum uncials which are dated in the fourth and fifth centuries: the Vatican, the Sinaitic, the Alexandrian, the Ephraem palimpsest manuscript, and Codex Bezae. These Greek manuscripts, along with numerous supporting uncials and cursives, provide the primary sources for the Greek New Testament. There are two types of secondary source-materials: the ancient versions or translations, and quotations made by the early Fathers. The most important early version in the East was the Syriac. The Syriac versions consist of the Old Syriac and the Peshitta, the latter being represented in more manuscripts while the former is the more important text-witness. The dominant version in the West was the Latin. Jerome's Latin Vulgate was the standard Bible of Western Europe for more than a thousand years. Its bearing on the original Greek text, however, is not as great as that of a few Old Latin copies. The writings of the early Fathers are of genuine value because of their frequent citations of the New Testament letters.

FOR CONSIDERATION

1. In this chapter two fifth century manuscripts are discussed. Name them. Which of these is a palimpsest manuscript? What is a palimpsest manuscript?

2. Explain what is meant by a lectionary manuscript. How does a lectionary compare in value with other manuscripts?

3. List some of the important Syriac manuscripts. Distinguish between the Old Syriac and the Peshitta Syriac.

4. Discuss the importance of the Latin witnesses, especially that of the Vulgate. Tell about Jerome's work on the Latin Vulgate.

5. Who are the early Fathers? In what ways can they help in providing knowledge for the New Testament text?

The Text of the New Testament

We have already seen that the original autographs of the New Testament are no longer in existence. We may wonder why the Supreme Governor of the world would allow this to happen. We may be tempted to ask why God did not in some way collect all of the original letters of the inspired writers and store them up through the years for safe keeping. Final answers to these questions cannot be given by men. Nevertheless we can see that it was necessary for *some* copies of the originals to be made, for otherwise there could have been no spreading of the written record; and we can also see that the first copies had to be made by use of the originals.

Yet problems arise and persist in the making of books. Today with modern printing methods it is not unusual to see glaring mistakes in published materials. Some of the greatest mistakes in the history of the Bible have occurred since the invention of printing. More than 300 errors in the first edition of the King James Bible were corrected in the second edition two years later. In our own time, despite all concentrated efforts to the contrary, the Revised Standard Version of 1946 and 1952 was not exempt from the plague of misprints.

If in modern times errors somehow appear in printed copies of the Bible, it is not difficult to see how mistakes slipped unnoticed into the New Testament manuscripts long ago. All ancient books had to be produced by hand, and no human hand is so exact or eye so sharp as to preclude the possibility of error. So errors were made; errors were copied; and errors were mixed in with the pure text.

Textual Criticism

The presence of these errors in the text of the Bible has given rise to a highly advanced science known as *Textual Criticism.* This science is also referred to as *Lower Criticism,* in contrast to what is called *Higher Criticism.* While Higher Criticism devotes itself to such things as the study of authorship, date of composition and historical value of a given Biblical document, Lower Criticism is concerned only with the form of words — the text — of that document.

The function of the textual critic is plain: he seeks by comparison and study of all the available evidence to recover the exact words of the author's original composition. The New Testament text-critic seeks, in short, to weed out the chaff of bad readings from the genuine Greek text. He realizes that his task is as important as the message which is borne in the text. Why is he so much concerned about the Greek text? Because he knows that the only way to have a reliable English translation is to make sure that the original fountain-head is free from all impurities. He realizes that if the Greek text is faulty, all translations from the Greek will likewise be at fault.

Mistakes of Copyists

It is now possible for us to look back over existent manuscripts and classify the types of mistakes made by the ancient scribe. Manuscript faults come about in two ways: either the alterations made by the scribe are unintentional slips of the pen, or else the alterations are made deliberately.

1. Unintentional Errors. Mistakes of the hand, eye and ear are of frequent occurrence in the manuscripts, but usually pose no problem because they are so easy to pick out. Often a scribe with a copy before him mistakes one word for another, and so by chance copies down the wrong word. Sometimes a scribe confuses words of similar sound, as in English we often interchange "affect" and "effect." Not a few times does the scribe, especially if he is unskilled in the language, misunderstand the passage due to improper division of the words. When the scribe does this we can sympathize with him, remembering that during most of the uncial period the style of writing was to crowd the letters to-

gether in such a way as to leave the words without intervening spaces between them.

Errors of omission and addition are common in all the manuscripts. Words sometimes are omitted by a copyist for no apparent reason, simply an unintentional omission. More often, however, omissions are due to the similar appearance of words at a corresponding point several lines above or below in the manuscript. The scribe's eye might skip, for example, from the end of line 6 to a similar word at the end of line 10. Likewise a scribe may add to his copy in the same way. He may inadvertently transcribe a word twice in succession. He may write, for example, "Jesus, Jesus" instead of simply "Jesus." Or instead of omitting several lines due to a similar word ending, he may copy these lines twice. But the textual critic by comparison of the many manuscripts can detect and explain these errors without hesitation.

Another form of error, more difficult to solve, grows out of the practice of writing explanatory notes in the margin. These marginal notes are somehow incorporated in the main body of material and thus become a part of the text. But it should be stressed in this connection that the New Testament manuscripts rarely exhibit this kind of error, and that when it does occur our many textual witnesses keep us on the right course.

2. Intentional Errors. Unintentional alterations in the manuscripts are many, but the vast majority of them are of little consequence. What presents a more serious problem to the textual critic are the variant readings which have been purposefully inserted by the scribe. We are not to think that these insertions were made by some dishonest scribe who simply wanted to tamper with the text. Almost always the intention of the scribe is good and he only wants to "correct" what appears to be an error in the text. This was often the case when a scribe was copying some portion of the Gospels. If he found a statement of Jesus in one Gospel similar to a statement in another, he would modify one in order that it be in perfect agreement with the other. This may be the explanation of a variant found in two verses of Matthew and Luke. The King James Version of Matthew 11:19 reads: "But wisdom is justified of her children," an exact parallel of Luke 7:35; but the more recent translations of

Matthew have "works" instead of "children," in agreement with our earliest manuscript authorities. We surmise that at some early date "works" was changed (deliberately?) by a copyist in harmony with Luke's Gospel and thus are practically certain that originally the two records of Jesus' sayings were not the same.

Basic Rules of Textual Criticism

The above textual variation (whether "children" or "works") may be approached in other ways. Over a period of several centuries Textual Criticism has formulated a number of fundamental "rules" or principles which have proved of inestimable value in deciding between variations in the manuscripts. These rules are not hard and fast, but only serve as general principles to guide and stabilize the textual critic.

With the above problem in mind, it is interesting to see what happens when some of the leading principles of Textual Criticism are followed. One basic rule is that the more difficult reading is to be preferred. At face value, without further explanation, this rule may be misleading. Obviously, some scribal errors of omission or addition scramble up the text to the extent of nonsense. When this is the case, if the more difficult reading is to be preferred, the text would be meaningless. Ruling out blunders of this kind, practically always the more difficult reading will prove to be the better reading. This is true because it was a natural tendency for the scribe to smooth out rough places in the text which he was copying. If a scribe looks at a passage which he does not understand, or at a word which is unfamiliar to him, he will think that somewhere along the line his text has become corrupt; in this event he will alter the passage slightly, thinking all the while that he is improving it. In Matthew 11:19, which reading is to be preferred, "children" or "works"? Which of the two is the more difficult reading? Undoubtedly the more difficult reading is "works," which leaves a difference of one word between Matthew and Luke.

Solving this question of one word in Matthew also serves to illustrate other important textual principles. In any given problem the *quality* of witnesses to the text is much more important than the *quantity*. Or, as it is often put, textual authorities must be weighed rather than counted. Thousands of manuscripts and versions may support a certain reading, but if they are of late date and stand opposed to the early uncials their witness is to be rejected. In the case of Matthew 11:19, what is the evidence from the manuscripts and versions? And where shall we go to find such information?

We shall attempt to answer the latter question briefly and then proceed in our original inquiry. If you are reading Matthew 11:19 in the American Standard Version, you will see a footnote which reads, "Many ancient authorities read *children*: as in Luke 7:35." This note is sufficient for most people; but if you are interested in finding out exactly how the ancient authorities read, you will need to go to a recent edition of Nestle's *New Testament in Greek*. Here you will find at the bottom of the page a series of abbreviations which indicates the textual authorities for and against "works" in Matthew 11:19.

What is the textual evidence on "children" and "works"? In favor of "children" are the Ephraem Manuscript and Codex Bezae (both from the fifth century), and almost all of the other later manuscripts; also the Old Syriac and all of the Latin versions. Against "children" and in support of "works" are the Vatican and Sinaitic Manuscripts (both from the fourth century), and a few other less important witnesses. This means that there are literally thousands of copies of manuscripts and versions which read "children" and only a handful that read "works." But the quality of witnesses is of more importance than the quantity. Unquestionably, the *quality* is in support of the reading "works," as found in the Vatican and Sinaitic Manuscripts. So because of the agreement of these two early uncials, all of the later translations read "works" for "children" in Matthew 11:19. Very often, as it happens here, the presence of the Vatican and Sinaitic Manuscripts in behalf of a reading is sufficient authority for that reading. This will illustrate the unchallenged supremacy which these two uncials sustain as witnesses on the New Testament text.

Still another important rule enters in here. In parallel texts, as we find in the Gospels, *different* readings are usually preferred. All of the Gospels present but one view of Jesus, that He is the Son of God. Yet in presenting this view their individual descriptions of Him and His sayings often employ different words. Through the years these verbal distinctions, either intentionally or unintentionally, would tend to be "harmonized" by the scribes. Thus it is a sound conclusion that in parallel accounts the text which preserves minute verbal differences is generally the better text. In our example of Matthew 11:19 the earliest manuscripts retain a verbal distinction between the two accounts. This is an added reason for believing that "works" is the preferable reading.

Naturally there are many other similar rules of Textual Criticism, some of which are much more technical in character. It is hoped that these few examples provide something of an insight into the mind of the textual critic. What an unexperienced person might consider a maze of bewildering data on the text, a trained specialist will regard as a wealth of material in which has been preserved the original reading — and in this belief and by means of exact principles he sets to work.

Summary

The New Testament books have been handed down to us by means of thousands of copies. Although God inspired the New Testament writers, He did not miraculously guide the hands of the copyists. Textual or Lower Criticism seeks to counteract inevitable scribal errors and recover the true form of the text. Many mistakes in the manuscripts crept into the text unintentionally, and are not difficult to detect. Other textual modifications were made intentionally, usually by a well-meaning scribe, and these do not stand out so clearly. Yet even then a textual critic is armed with a multitude of aids to help him overcome the problem. In a case like Matthew 11:19 "works" is a better reading than "children" because: (1) the quality of witnesses is more important than the quantity, (2) the more difficult reading is to be preferred, and (3) the different reading in parallel passages is usually the more reliable one. These are but a few illustrations of the many sound principles upon which Textual Criticism is based. Since Textual Criticism is a sound science, our text is secure and our faith remains unshakable.

For Consideration

1. What is the task of Textual Criticism? Is it to be identified with Lower or Higher Criticism?
2. List some ways in which unintentional mistakes may be made in the manuscripts. What are some examples of intentional variations? Of the two groups, which presents the more difficult problem for the textual critic?
3. Review and discuss some of the main rules of Textual Criticism.
4. How is it possible that the authority of a few manuscripts can outweigh the testimony of many witnesses? What could be the result if this rule were not followed?

X

6

Significance of
Textual Variations

It is a fact that the New Testament text has been transmitted to us through the hands of copyists. It is also a fact that since these hands were human they were susceptible to the slips and faults of all human hands. It is not true, therefore, that God has guided the many different scribes as they executed their tasks of copying the Sacred Scriptures. The Scriptures, although divine, have been handed down through the centuries by means of copies, just like any other book. A failure to recognize this would make it necessary for God to perform a miracle every time a scribe picked up pen and ink. And this assumption is almost inconceivable!

Number of Variations

Suppose someone were to say that there are 200,000 errors in the New Testament text. What would be our response? Is this a correct figure? And if so, how can we be sure that we have the original New Testament message?

From one point of view it may be said that there are 200,000 scribal errors in the manuscripts, but it is wholly misleading and untrue to say that there are 200,000 errors in the text of the New Testament. This large number is gained by counting all the variations in all of the manuscripts (about 4,500). This means that if, for example, one word is misspelled in 4,000 different manuscripts, it amounts to 4,000 "errors." Actually in a case of this kind only one slight error has been made and it has been copied 4,000 times. But this is the procedure which is followed in arriving at the large number of 200,000 "errors." A person is either unlearned or of a skeptical mind who tries to take this large number of variations and use it in such a way as to undermine one's faith in the Word of God.

In this connection one other fact needs to be emphasized. This large number of variations exists in exact proportion to the number of manuscripts which we possess. There are far more copies of the New Testament than of any other book from the ancient world. Because we have more New Testament manuscripts, we have more variations. Suppose we had only ten manuscripts of the New Testament. In so few manuscripts the total number of variations would be small. But if we had only ten manuscripts, the New Testament text would not stand on as sound a ground as it otherwise does. *If the large number of manuscripts increases the total of variations, it supplies at the same time the means of checking them.*

Consequences of Variations

What about the significance of these variations? Are these variations immaterial or are they important? What bearing do they have on the New Testament message and faith? To respond to these questions it will be helpful to introduce three types of textual variations, classified in relation to their significance for our present New Testament text.

1. Trivial variations which are of no consequence to the text. The great majority of variant readings in the manuscripts has to do with trivial matters, many of them so minute that they cannot be represented in translation. Perhaps the best way to demonstrate this is to open at random a page of the Greek text. Let us take the same page which was consulted previously in order to learn the evidence pro and con for the reading "works" in Matthew 11:19. On this small page thirteen verses (Matt. 11:10-23) appear. A quick look at the bottom of the page shows that nine variant readings are listed. At first glance nine variants out of thirteen verses seem alarming. Yet every other variant on the page, besides "children" or "works," is trivial in nature. Five of the variants concern the omission or addition of such words as "for," "and," "the," etc., and the others have to do simply with different forms of the same Greek words. At no point is there a real problem of the text, except with the alternative of "chil-

dren" and "works," which as we have seen is rather easily resolved.

This page of variants is truly typical of the mistakes found in our copies. Very often words in the Greek copies are spelled slightly differently over a period of years. This is not surprising, especially when we recall how much English words have changed their spelling the last few centuries. One has only to take in hand a copy of the first edition of the King James Bible of 1611 and he will quickly see what a great change a few centuries have made on the form of English words — and these changes have occurred since the printing press supposedly standardized the English language. In a similar way the Greek language was undergoing change, and the natural thing for the scribe to do was to alter the spelling of certain words in keeping with the accepted standards of his day. Variations in grammar and even vocabulary are to be explained on the same basis. Or a variation may be no more than a change in the order of words, as "the Lord Jesus Christ" instead of "Christ Jesus the Lord." In all cases like this we have an abundance of information which enables us, even in trivial matters, to make a concrete decision as to the original text. Even if we did not have this information, if we were left completely in the dark in reference to such things as spelling and word-order, still we would not be in danger of losing the Divine Revelation.

2. Substantial variations which are of no consequence to the text. We do not wish to leave the impression that all textual variants can be lightly dismissed. Some variations involve not only a word or two, but a whole verse or even several verses. Certainly variations of this kind are more than trivial. It should be hastily added, however, that these variations of a substantial character do not affect our present text. They do not affect our text today because they are not supported by the most authoritative textual witnesses.

A few examples will clarify what we mean. Codex Bezae of the fifth century has already been discussed. (Cf. Chapter 4.) This manuscript often has peculiar readings, one of which is found in Luke 6:5: "On the same day, seeing one working on the sabbath day, he said unto him, Man, if you know what you are doing, you are blessed; but if you do not know, you are accursed and a transgressor of the law." This curious incident is recorded in no other manuscript or version. It is beyond doubt a substantial variation, but we are sure that it was not a part of Luke's original Gospel. It in no way changes our text because modern Textual Criticism has unhesitatingly rejected it.

A more familiar passage found in our early English translations also illustrates the same principle. The story of the adulterous woman (John 7:53—8:11) involves a number of verses and clearly represents a substantial variation. Almost all recent translations do not include this account in the main body of their texts. The American Standard Version separates it from the main narrative and encloses it in brackets, indicating doubt in the minds of the translators concerning it. The Revised Standard Version puts this story in a footnote. Both translations briefly explain to their readers the reasons for their actions.

Why have these later translations looked with suspicion on these verses? The answer is simple: no early manuscript, except one, and practically none of the early versions have the story of the adulterous woman in them. The one early manuscript which contains the story is the very one (Codex Bezae) that is known for its peculiar readings, as we have seen above in Luke 6:5. Otherwise, it is necessary to come down to manuscripts of the eighth century and later before the story is found again. In addition, some of the manuscripts that have it also have notes of doubt in the margin concerning it; others put it at the end of the Gospel of John; and still others insert it in the Gospel of Luke, after Luke 21:38. Certainly there were grave doubts all along concerning this passage. But do these past doubts place our text in a questionable atmosphere? Indeed they do not. Just as we accept the reading "works" instead of "children" (Matt. 11:19) on the evidence of the early manuscripts, so here on the basis of the early manuscripts we do not include the adulterous woman story in our text. Where did the story come from? No one knows, but it was probably a tradition handed down from the primitive church. Our early manuscripts do not deny the truthfulness of the story — its truthfulness is an open question — but attest that the story was not an original part of John's Gospel.

Another passage of interest is found in Acts 8:37. The King James translation of this verse reads: "And Philip said, if thou believest with all thine heart, thou mayest. And he answered and said, I believe that Jesus Christ is the Son of God." These words are represented as a part of a conversation between Philip the Evangelist and the eunuch at the time of the eunuch's baptism. These are familiar words, stressing the importance of faith in Jesus Christ. Yet these words are not found in either the American Standard or the Revised Standard Versions. These recent translations, on the basis of the evidence, are compelled to omit this verse from the book of Acts. It is true that a seventh century uncial, some good cursive manuscripts and the Old Latin Version support the verse, but practically all the other manuscripts and versions stand opposed to it. Because no Greek manuscript earlier than the seventh century knows of this reading, beyond doubt it could not have formed a part of the original account of Acts.

The case of I John 5:7 is less complex. The King James Version reads: "For there are three that bear record in heaven, the Father, the Word, and the Holy Ghost: and these three are one." An interesting circumstance led to the introduction of this verse in the English Bible. After the invention of printing the first person to publish an edition of the printed Greek text was a man by the name of Erasmus. His first edition came out in the year of 1516. But the first and second editions of Erasmus did not include I John 5:7. A mild controversy was stirred up because the verse was indisputably in the late Latin copies. Erasmus insisted that his text was right, and was so sure of himself that he rashly promised to include the verse in his text if one single Greek copy could be found in support of it. At length a copy turned up, and Erasmus true to his word put the verse into the third edition of his Greek Testament. William Tyndale was the first man to translate the New Testament into English based on a Greek text (instead of Latin) ; and it was Erasmus' third edition which he employed in making his translation. So from Tyndale down to the King James Bible, I John 5:7 has been a part of English Scripture.

The textual evidence is all against I John 5:7. Of all the Greek manuscripts, there are only two which contain it. These two manuscripts are of very late dates, one from the fourteenth or fifteenth century and the other from the sixteenth century. Both clearly show this verse to be translated from the Latin.

These are examples of significant variations, but actually they do not have a bearing on our text today. They do not affect our text simply because there is not enough evidence for them to have an effect. Thus the American Standard Version, which habitually makes explanation when its text varies from the King James, does not so much as note I John 5:7 in its margin and instead rearranges the verse structure. I John 5:7, Acts 8:37, and John 7:53—8:11 reflect substantial variations in some manuscripts, but since they are unknown in the early uncials they cannot cast doubt on our improved text today.

3. Substantial variations which have bearing on the text. It remains now to consider a group of textual readings which at some points raises questions about our text. It would be a simple task to ignore these things. But facts are facts, and our ignorance of them solves no problems.

Of interest to all, and a passage which well illustrates textual variations which affect our text, are the twelve verses at the end of Mark's Gospel. If one looks carefully at the American Standard Version he notices that these last verses are set apart from the main text of Mark. The new translation of the Revised Standard Version puts these verses in a footnote and also gives another ending to Mark as found in some manuscripts. All of this, of course, indicates that there is some doubt about the conclusion of Mark's work.

The problem of Mark 16 is rather unique. In the cases of I John 5:7 and John 7:53—8:11 there really is no problem — all the authoritative evidence looks in one direction. But this is not the case with Mark 16 — the evidence apparently looks in two directions. The evidence against Mark 16:9-20 mostly rests on the Vatican and Sinaitic Manuscripts. These two uncials of the fourth century are our very best manuscripts, and as textual witnesses are acknowledged as being in a class by themselves. We are thus confronted with the problem that the two manuscripts which we rely upon most do not have these closing verses of Mark. There is additional significant evidence against Mark 16, including the witness of the earliest known manuscript of the Old Syriac.

In favor of Mark 16:9-20 there are a host of witnesses: the Alexandrian Manuscript, the Ephraem Manuscript, Codex Bezae, other early uncials, all late uncials and cursives, five old Latin authorities plus the Vulgate, one Old Syriac manuscript, the Syriac Peshitta version, and many other versions. Besides, there is a plain statement from Irenaeus (early Christian writer) which clearly shows the existence of Mark 16:9-20 in the second century and the belief that Mark was its author.

In brief this is the negative and positive data on the question. On one hand is the unparalleled reliability of the Vatican and Sinaitic Manuscripts; on the other hand is almost all of the other evidence. J. W. McGarvey wrote a capable defense of Mark 16:9-20 in his *Commentary on Matthew and Mark*. It was first published, however, in 1875, before the great work of West-cott and Hort on the Greek text was completed. Yet McGarvey's position, with a few minor modifications, can stand with credit today. But the problem persists: What about the negative evidence of the Vatican and Sinaitic Manuscripts?

Whatever the correct view, it is important to note that the truthfulness of this passage is not in dispute. The main events of Mark 16:9-20 are recorded elsewhere, so at any rate we are not in danger of forfeiting heavenly treasure. The variant readings in the manuscripts are not of such a nature that threaten to overthrow our faith. Except for a few rare instances we have an unquestioned text, and even then one principle of faith or command of the Lord is not involved. Further assurances concerning our text will be studied in the next chapter.

Summary

A large number of variations do exist in the manuscripts, but this number is ascertained by counting all the variants in all the manuscripts. When this is understood the large figure of textual differences does not seem frightening. Most variations are made up of minute details, either obvious scribal blunders or slight changes in spelling, grammar, and word-order. These are of no consequence to our text. Other variations might have considerable weight on our text, but they are not supported by the early textual authorities. A few variations present problems for our text, but all of them are not impossible to solve. Even if they were, since the number of them is so few, these should not be stumbling blocks to our faith.

For Consideration

1. How would you explain such a large number (200,000) of variations in the New Testament manuscripts? How is this large number derived?
2. Give some examples of trivial variations.
3. Why do recent translations of the Bible not include: (a) the story of the adulterous woman, and (b) Acts 8:37, and (c) I John: 5:7?
4. What is the textual problem of Mark 16? Should the ending of Mark prove to be a hindrance to our faith? Why?

7

Restoring the
New Testament Text

The New Testament text has been borne through the centuries by means of manuscripts and other materials. In the transmission of the text mistakes were bound to appear. Our primary concern, however, is the bearing that these mistakes have on the text. The conclusion reached in the foregoing study is that practically all of the variations found among the manuscripts do not affect our present text. We are now ready to learn more about our accepted text, something of how it came about, and the effect recent discoveries have had on it.

Our modern Greek text may be described as a reconstructed or restored text. There are only two alternatives open if we seek to print a Greek text: either we can select one manuscript and make it the standard text, or we can consult a number of manuscripts and authorities and by comparison reconstruct a text which we feel is like the original. If we choose the former course we are destined to failure, for no one manuscript is free from obvious scribal errors. If we choose the latter course we will be assured of getting much closer to the original New Testament autographs. For this reason the latter course has always been followed in the printing of the Greek New Testament. This means that our modern-type text is an *edition* of the New Testament text restored through all the aids of Textual Criticism.

Authorities for Restoring the Text

Let us suppose that we do not have a modern edition of the New Testament text. What sources shall we use in restoring the primitive text? The answer to this question will be given briefly and will partially serve as a review of the last four chapters.

1. Manuscripts. The first and primary source of information in restoring the text are manuscripts of the original language, which for the New Testament would be Greek manuscripts. But all manuscripts are not of equal weight, and therefore some may be classified as good, others as better, and a few as best. Further study of these manuscripts shows that some habitually agree in their readings. They are evidently derived from a common ancestor and are called a "family." These families of manuscripts have arisen at different times and under varying conditions. Within certain limits, their origins can be traced back to different quarters of the world: some to Alexandria in Egypt and are known as "Alexandrian"; others to Antioch of Syria, designated as "Syrian" or "Byzantine"; and still others to Western Europe, which are termed "Western"; and so on. Since these various groups represent the wide range of textual variants, it is safe to conclude that whenever several important families agree on a given reading, this amounts to textual certainty.

2. Versions. The Bible was translated by early Christians into many tongues. Surely these translations, especially the early ones, will provide much helpful information. These translations had to be made from some type of Greek text, and to find out what type of text each represents provides us with an independent line of witnesses.

3. The Fathers. Early Christians wrote extensively about their religion and quoted frequently from their sacred writings. Not a few of their quotations give us the exact words of their Biblical texts. These quotations not only supply many of the words of their Scriptures, but they also reveal what kind of text was in existence in the second and third centuries.

The manuscripts, the versions, citations from the various Fathers — these are the tools available when we undertake to restore the primitive text of the New Testament. Using these tools with discretion, it is possible to come so near the original autographs that we can all but grasp them in our hands.

The Westcott-Hort Text

In the year 1881 two Cambridge scholars, B. F. Westcott and

F. J. A. Hort, jointly published a completely revised edition of the New Testament text. This publication was in two volumes; one contained the text itself and the other comprised various notes on selected textual readings, together with a monumental discussion of the principles underlying their work.

It is scarcely possible to overstate the significance of this new text. Thirty years of exacting labor had been given by Westcott and Hort to this project. Their achievement was revolutionary not so much because of new ideas, but rather because of the deliberate thoroughness of their work and the unquestioned soundness of the principles which backed it up. No piece of evidence had been passed over unnoticed, no authority had not been brought into proper perspective. Basically, the Westcott-Hort text represented a wholesale rejection of mass authorities and an acknowledged dependence on the Sinaitic and Vatican Manuscripts, particularly the Vatican. Time has but confirmed their immense contribution to the status of our New Testament text.

In the same year of 1881 the English Revised Version of the New Testament appeared. The deserved attention given to this great revision brought added acclaim to the Westcott-Hort text. While the new translation was not strictly based on the Westcott-Hort edition, nevertheless Westcott and Hort had served as the best-informed textual scholars on the Revision Committee. Naturally their influence on the Committee was a dominant factor in determining the final form of the text, as is shown by the new kind of text in the revision. The Westcott-Hort text, along with the new translation, dealt the final blow to the old type of text (Received Text) upon which the King James Version is based.

The Effect of Recent Discoveries

Since the work of Westcott and Hort was completed in 1881, what is the status of the New Testament text today? What has been the effect of recently discovered materials on our restored text? Do these discoveries oppose or confirm the work of Westcott and Hort?

The amazing finds of the last half-century or more provide one of the most interesting links in the long chain of the Bible's history. Our world is not standing still. Many people who are aware of this in terms of material advancements are completely unaware that great things are also turning up in the world of Biblical knowledge. Some of these important discoveries will now be noted.

1. Sinaitic Syriac Manuscript. In 1892 two sisters, Mrs. Agnes S. Lewis and Mrs. Margaret D. Gibson, made a significant discovery. These Cambridge ladies had come to the monastery of St. Catherine on Mt. Sinai in quest of rare Biblical manuscripts. It will be remembered that it was here at St. Catherine's where Tischendorf had made his astounding discovery; and it was here also, even after Tischendorf's visits, that other important manuscript recoveries had been made. In pursuit of their task Mrs. Lewis and Mrs. Gibson examined a number of manuscripts, one of which was an old palimpsest document. The layer of writing underneath was identified by Mrs. Lewis as being a Syriac copy of the Gospels, and subsequent studies of the manuscript have shown it to be a representative of the Old Syriac translation. In fact, the Sinaitic Syriac is the earliest known copy of the Old Syriac, reaching back to the fifth or possibly to the fourth century. One item of interest is that it does not contain Mark 16:9-20.

2. The Washington Manuscript. In 1906 a group of Biblical manuscripts was acquired by Charles L. Freer of Detroit. The most important document of this group is a copy of the Four Gospels dating from the fourth or fifth century. One of its interesting features concerns the close of Mark's Gospel. The questioned verses are found in this codex, but in the middle of the verses (after vs. 14) is an interpolation of several lines unknown in other manuscripts. Yet it is a valuable witness on the Gospels, one of a few early manuscripts located in the United States (Washington, D.C.).

3. Koridethi Gospels. This manuscript became known in 1913. Although it is of a late date (about ninth century), it has received much attention in recent studies due to its generous contribution of information regarding a type of text of which it is the chief representative. Its discovery is one of the more significant developments for textual study in recent years.

4. Chester Beatty Papyri. On November 17, 1931, Sir Frederic Kenyon, Director of the British Museum, made an announce-

ment in a news article of one of the most amazing discoveries of the twentieth century. Indeed, the discovery has often been described as the most important gain for New Testament text-criticism since Tischendorf announced the discovery of the Sinaitic Codex. A group of papyri, said to have come from jars taken out of an Egyptian graveyard, had been acquired by a well-known manuscript collector, A. Chester Beatty. In addition to Mr. Beatty's collection, other parts of the same group were acquired by the University of Michigan and by private individuals. In all there are portions of twelve manuscripts. Nine of these contain parts of the Old Testament in Greek: considerable portions of Genesis, Numbers and Deuteronomy, and parts of Esther, Ezekiel and Daniel. Three manuscripts in the group are of the New Testament books.

The first of these New Testament manuscripts is known as P45 (P standing for Papyrus). It contains portions of thirty leaves of the Gospels and Acts (two leaves from Matthew, six of Mark, seven of Luke, two of John, and thirteen of Acts). Although to some extent fragmentary, this codex is of inestimable value since it dates from the third century or earlier.

The second manuscript (P46) is a remarkable collection of the Pauline epistles. It is more than a fragment, for it contains eighty-six leaves out of an original 104. The order of the letters included is: Romans, Hebrews, I and II Corinthians, Ephesians, Galatians, Philippians, Colossians, I and II Thessalonians. The manuscript is usually dated in the beginning of the third century. Of all the manuscripts available on the Bible text, P46 is unquestionably one of the most important. It is very old, of course, but it is also very accurate. Its text is of such high quality that it ranks with the Vatican and Sinaitic Codices.

The third New Testament manuscript of the group (P47) consists of ten leaves from the middle section of the book of Revelation. It is likewise dated from about the third century.

5. John Rylands Fragment (P52). This is only a fragment (3½ by 2½ inches) and would hardly deserve mention except for the fact that it is the oldest known manuscript of any part of the New Testament. Written on both sides, it contains a few verses of the Gospel of John (John 18:31-33, 37, 38). It was originally obtained in 1920 by the famous papyrologist Dr. B. P.

Grenfell, but it was sometime later before Mr. C. H. Roberts made positive identification of it. Acquired for the John Rylands Library of Manchester, England, it remains there today. As to its date, it is confidently assigned to the first half of the second century. How it could be wished that we had more than a fragment; yet it gives undeniable evidence on the circulation of John's Gospel in Egypt, where it was found, only a few years after it was written. It forevermore answers the view once held that John's Gospel was not written until the middle of the second century. Also, it is important to note that although this papyrus piece contains only a few verses, these verses from the second century are precisely like our text 1800 years later.

6. Papyrus Bodmer II (P[66]). As late as 1956 Victor Martin, a professor of classical philology at the University of Geneva, published a papyrus codex of the Gospel of John. It is known as Papyrus Bodmer II because it is a part of the famous Bodmer Library of World Literature at Geneva. The details of the manuscript's discovery are as yet unknown. The publication in 1956 by Professor Martin included the bulk of the manuscript, Chapters 1:1 through 14:26, except for two missing leaves from the sixth chapter; and since that time, in 1958, the fragmentary contents of the remaining chapters have been produced. Papyrus Bodmer II is dated about A.D. 200. It is a weighty witness indeed, probably the oldest book in substantial condition of the New Testament.

These are examples of some of the fascinating stories about the New Testament which have been transpiring in recent years. The question is, what effect do these extraordinary developments have on our present New Testament text?

Discoveries made since the time of Westcott and Hort have revealed a number of things, but these discoveries taken as a whole confirm the Westcott-Hort type of text and stand opposed to the older type of text. A good illustration of this is the last mentioned papyrus codex, dating perhaps back to the second century. This text is remarkably like the great uncials, the Sinaitic and the Vatican. It does not have the peculiar readings of the Codex Bezae, nor those of the later manuscripts. In agreement with the American Standard and Revised Standard Versions, it does not have the verse about the angel troubling the water

(John 5:4). The story of the adulterous woman (John 7:53 — 8:11), which was considered in the preceding study, likewise is not found in the early papyrus. Discoveries of this kind make us more certain than ever before of the reliability of our modern text; and in view of the past, where the Westcott-Hort type of text has been confirmed again and again, it is not to be anticipated that future discoveries will greatly alter the New Testament text. Other discoveries will indeed be made, but we expect them to point in the same direction.

Our conclusion is that the text of the New Testament rests on solid foundations. A great part of the New Testament text has never been questioned. Westcott and Hort in the beginning of their work take extreme care in giving assurance concerning the reliability of our text. They say: "The proportion of words virtually accepted on all hands as raised above doubt is very great, not less, on a rough computation, than seven-eighths of the whole. The remaining eighth therefore, formed in great part by changes of order and other comparative trivialities, constitutes the whole area of criticism." They conclude by saying that "the amount of what can in any sense be called substantial variation is but a small fraction of the whole residuary variation, and can hardly form more than a thousandth part of the entire text. Since there is reason to suspect that an exaggerated impression prevails as to the extent of possible textual corruption in the New Testament . . . we desire to make it clearly understood beforehand how much of the New Testament stands in no need of a textual critic's labours."[1]

Here the greatest of textual critics tell us that many people *exaggerate* textual differences, and that only a thousandth part of the New Testament represents substantial variation! We might add that even where "substantial variation" may exist, not a single principle of faith or divine command is involved.

Sir Frederic Kenyon, Director of the British Museum for twenty-one years, often expressed his confidence on the wholesome condition of the New Testament text. He once wrote: "The

---

[1]B. F. Westcott and F. J. A. Hort, *The New Testament in the Original Greek*. Introduction and Appendix. (Cambridge: University Press, 1881), pp. 2-3.

Christian can take the whole Bible in his hand and say without fear or hesitation that he holds in it the true word of God, handed down without essential loss from generation to generation throughout the centuries."[2]

Summary

Our New Testament text of today is a reconstructed or restored text. It has been reconstructed by modern scholarship from three independent lines of witnesses: the manuscripts, the versions, and the quotations found in the writings of the Fathers. A great epoch of textual advance was marked by the publication in 1881 of a revised Greek text. This restored text was edited by Westcott and Hort and holds today, eighty years later, a first-rate position in its field. In more recent times many significant discoveries have been made which touch upon the text of the New Testament. The most important of these discoveries are the papyri, some of which are more than a century earlier than the celebrated Vatican and Sinaitic Manuscripts. Yet all of these discoveries confirm the type of text produced by Westcott and Hort.

---

[2]*Our Bible and the Ancient Manuscripts.* Revised by A. W. Adams. (New York: Harper and Brothers, 1958), p. 55.

FOR CONSIDERATION

1. What three main sources are available to us in restoring the original text of the New Testament? Which is the most important source?
2. Name the two textual scholars who produced a completely revised edition of the Greek text. When was their work published? What other famous publication came out in the same year?
3. List some of the important recent discoveries that give added light to the New Testament text.
4. Briefly tell about the Chester Beatty papyri.
5. What is the oldest known fragment of the New Testament text? Discuss the significance of this fragment as to the text and date of authorship of the Gospel of John.
6. How recent would a translation have to be in order to profit from the revised text of Westcott and Hort and from the Biblical discoveries mentioned in this chapter?

8

The Text of the Old Testament

In the preceding chapters we have spoken in some detail about the transmission of the Greek text of the New Testament. Again it is essential to stress the importance of the Greek text, for without the words of the Greek text we are left without a foundation upon which our English translations rest. There can be no reliable English version unless there is an accurate Greek text. But we have seen that no serious objection can be laid against our Greek text, which means that our faith based on the New Testament message stands secure.

Our next task is to focus attention upon the text of the Old Testament. It will not be necessary to go at length into the question of the Old Testament text, for the principles followed in the restoration of the New Testament text largely apply to that of the Old.

Text-data for the Old Testament is not vast as compared with the multitude of witnesses on the Greek text, nor does the available data appear as impressive. Manuscripts of the New Testament date back to the fourth century, and several papyri documents reach back even farther. Extant materials on the Old Testament, however, are not as old. The earliest Hebrew manuscripts are known as the Cairo Codex and the Leningrad Codex of the Prophets. The Cairo Codex includes the Former and Latter Prophets and is dated at A.D. 895. The Leningrad Codex of the Prophets is slightly later, dating from A.D. 916. Another early Hebrew manuscript is the British Museum Codex of the Pentateuch. It has proved to be a very important witness on the Old Testament text, yet it comes from the tenth or eleventh century.

The oldest known manuscript of the entire Old Testament is the Leningrad Codex which was completed in 1008 A.D. Many other manuscripts, of course, are in existence, but these are the basic witnesses to the text of the Old Testament. The latest edition of the current Hebrew Bible (Kittel's *Biblia Hebraica*) is based on these four Hebrew manuscripts, in particular the Leningrad Codex of the complete Old Testament.

One may wonder why copies of the Hebrew Bible are late in comparison with the New Testament materials and especially so when it is recalled that the Old Testament was completed several centuries before the first New Testament book was written. The answer is not difficult to find. The Jewish scribes looked upon their copies of the Scriptures with an almost superstitious respect, which led them to give a ceremonial burial to any copy which was old or became worn. Their motive was to prevent the improper use of the material on which the sacred name of God had been inscribed. But however noble their intentions, this ancient custom has deprived us of the early Hebrew manuscripts which we might otherwise have, and thus has lengthened the gap between the available copies of the text and the Old Testament autographs.

The Massoretes

Before considering the present status of the Old Testament text, it will be necessary to say a little more about its background. Until the invention of printing, the Old Testament Scriptures were handed down to us by copying. This process makes it inevitable for scribal variations to appear. Especially is this the case with the Hebrew manuscripts, because of the difficulty of the language involved. Not a few letters of the Hebrew alphabet look very much alike, which sometimes led to the confusion of small details in the text. A good illustration of this is the familiar name Nebuchadrezzar, a form which is technically more accurate than the more familiar Nebuchadnezzar. The two names obviously refer to the same person, but a mixup of the similar Hebrew letters r and n occasioned this difference.

Recognizing the ever present possibility of scribal mistakes, and possessed with an almost inherent obsession to guard the letter of the law, there sprang up at an early date various circles of

Jewish scholars dedicated to the preservation of the Old Testament text. At the head of the list was a group of scribes centered at Tiberias, who are generally known as the *Massoretes*. Their school was not by any means the earliest, since it did not come into being until about 500 A.D., but it is the most important one for the history of the Hebrew text.

The Massoretes are so named because of their acknowledged dependence on the authoritative traditions *(Massorah)* concerning the text. Their labors are spread out over a period of four or five centuries and their contributions are many. They are perhaps best known for their system of vowels and accents which they devised for the Hebrew text. It will be remembered that all the letters in the Hebrew alphabet are consonants. Thus the Old Testament was first written without vowels. Although this may seem strange and crude to us, it was sufficient for the many centuries in which Hebrew continued as a spoken language. When eventually Hebrew was no longer spoken, the danger was eminent that the proper pronunciation of the words of the text would likewise disappear. To meet this danger the Massoretes, on the basis of their well kept traditions, inserted vowel points above and below the lines of the text. It must be emphasized, however, that they did not bother the text itself — they only added a means by which to insure the correct pronunciation of the text.

The Massoretes were not concerned only with such things as details of proper pronunciation. More than this, they sought ways and methods by which they could eliminate scribal slips of addition or omission. This they achieved through intricate procedures of counting. They numbered the verses, words and letters of each book. They counted the number of times each letter was used in each book. They noted verses which contained all the letters of the alphabet, or a certain number of them, etc. They calculated the middle verse, the middle word, and the middle letter of each book. (The middle verse of the Pentateuch is Leviticus 8:7, while the middle verse of the Hebrew Bible is Jeremiah 6:7.) Some of these notations can still be found in our printed Hebrew Bibles. With these safeguards, and others, when a scribe finished making a copy of a book he could then check the accuracy of his work before using it.

This briefly illustrates why the work of the Massoretes is so important. The Massoretes were textual critics of the first rank. They examined and appraised carefully all the textual materials available to them, and on the basis of their abundant evidence set down in writing the form of the text which had been received at least several centuries before their time. Indeed, their labors were so productive and their contributions so large that our Hebrew text today is often referred to as "the Massoretic text." The extant Hebrew manuscripts noted above are outstanding specimens of the Massoretic text.

Other Materials on the Text

The most important materials in the establishing of a text are those that are found in the original language of the text. The basic sources then of the Old Testament text will always remain the Hebrew manuscripts. Nevertheless additional materials are often in a position to throw much light on the traditional text. These materials are witnesses on the text in their own right and prove helpful in several ways. First, they tell us something of the kind of text in use prior to the time of the Massoretes, for some of these materials go even as far back as several centuries B.C. Second, these materials when used with discretion can even supply the missing words of the Massoretic text when it is obviously defective. On occasions the Revised Standard Version of 1952 has thought this necessary. In Genesis 4:8 the Revised Standard translation gives the words of Cain as, "Let us go out to the field." These words are added, as the footnote explains, in agreement with the united witness of the Samaritan Pentateuch and the Greek, Syriac and Latin translations. The Hebrew text at this point is apparently incomplete. Third, these materials with their parallel readings most often substantiate the Massoretic text and give to it an increased credibility. These additional textual authorities will now be noted.

1. Samaritan Pentateuch. The Samaritan Pentateuch is not a translation, but is a form of the Hebrew text itself. Its beginning is to be traced back to about 400 B.C. when the Samaritans separated themselves from the Jews and built their sanctuary on Mt. Gerizim, near Shechem. As a result the Samaritans adopted

their own form of the Hebrew Scriptures and counted as authoritative only the five books of Moses.

In one sense the Samaritan Pentateuch presents a problem, for it bears some 6,000 variants from the Massoretic text. But on examination the problem is not as great as it might appear. Most of the variants have to do with spelling and grammatical differences which do not affect the message of the text, while a number of others unmistakably have been inserted to support the peculiar beliefs of the Samaritan community. Over all there are few major differences between the Hebrew and Samaritan Pentateuchs, which means that to a high degree the Samaritan Pentateuch confirms the traditional Hebrew text.

2. Septuagint. The word "Septuagint" is derived from the Latin *Septuaginta,* meaning "Seventy," and is the common name given to the Greek translation of the Old Testament. According to an unfounded tradition, about seventy men took part in the translation of the Pentateuch. As the tradition goes, reported in the Letter of Aristeas, Jewish scholars from Jerusalem were summoned to Alexandria by the Egyptian king to make a translation from the Hebrew to the Greek. The translation when completed was to be placed in the famed library at Alexandria.

Little of the story is accepted as factual. It is believed that the version was completed at Alexandria, but probably by Alexandrian rather than Palestinian Jews. The time of the Egyptian king, Ptolemy II Philadelphus, is also probably right, making the origin of the Septuagint approximately 250 B.C. At a later date, time and circumstances unknown, the remaining books of the Old Testament were translated into Greek.

Whatever mysteries may surround it, the Septuagint translation will always hold interest among Christians. For a while it was the only Bible for the early church. It was the text most often quoted by the apostles and inspired writers of the New Testament. Yet beyond these prevailing attachments, the Septuagint version is an extremely valuable authority on the Old Testament text. It is true that it has its deficiencies; it has its mistakes of translation and its differences from the Massoretic text; — but still it plays a significant role in supporting the text of the Old Testament. While the Samaritan Pentateuch covers only the first five books, the Septuagint witness spans the remainder of the Old Testament as well.

3. Aramaic Targums. After the period of the Jewish exile, Aramaic began to be the spoken language of the Jews. In order for the people to understand the reading of the Scriptures in public worship, it was necessary that they be translated or paraphrased in Aramaic. The translation was called *targum*. By the time of the fifth century A.D. two official Targums had emerged, *Targum Onkelos* of the Pentateuch and *Targum Jonathan* of the prophets. Of the two, Targum Onkelos is considered the greater authority. Both are deliberately literal in their efforts of translation.

4. Syriac Peshitta. The Syriac translation was begun very early, perhaps as early as the middle of the first century A.D. In its earliest form the Peshitta is in close agreement with the Massoretic text. Later, there is considerable evidence where it has been unduly influenced by readings of the Septuagint. Nevertheless the Peshitta is an important tool in the text-criticism of the Old Testament.

5. Latin Versions and Others. There are two main types of the Latin translations, the Old Latin and the Vulgate. The Old Latin dates back to A.D. 150, but it has definite limitations because it is a translation based on the Septuagint. The Latin Vulgate, on the other hand, even though later, is a valuable text-authority. It was the work of the knowledgeable Jerome, who spent the years of 390-405 translating directly from the Hebrew into the Latin. At a time when all other translations of the Church resorted to the Septuagint, it was an unheard of thing to do! Jerome's work indeed has its short-comings, but even so it throws much light on the early Hebrew text.

Additional materials on the Old Testament text are available. There are such sources as the Biblical quotations found in the Talmud (200-500 A.D.), along with other Jewish materials; recently discovered fragments of Origen's Old Testament (Hexapla) in use in the third century A.D.; and still other versions such as the Coptic, the Ethiopic, the Armenian, and the Arabic. While all of these are not of equal importance for the text, they serve to illustrate the abundance of text-materials accessible outside the Hebrew manuscripts.

Present Status of Our Text

We have seen that our earliest Hebrew manuscripts date no farther back than the ninth century, which leaves a rather wide separation of centuries between the original Old Testament autographs and the materials available to us today. This might give occasion for alarm were it not for the extreme care taken by Jewish scribes as they made their copies of the Scriptures. Centuries prior to the Massoretes Jewish scribes were conscientiously seeking perfection in the transcription of the text. Evidence of this is found in the Talmud (Jewish civil and religious law) where rigid regulations are laid down for the preparation of copies of the Pentateuch to be used in the synagogues. "A synagogue roll must be written on the skins of clean animals, prepared for the particular use of the synagogue by a Jew. These must be fastened together with strings taken from clean animals. Every skin must contain a certain number of columns, equal throughout the entire codex. The length of each column must not extend over less than forty-eight, or more than sixty lines; and the breadth must consist of thirty letters. The whole copy must be first lined; and if three words be written in it without a line, it is worthless. The ink should be black, neither red, green, nor any other colour and be prepared according to a definite recipe. An *authentic* copy must be the exemplar, from which the transcriber ought not in the least to deviate. No word or letter, not even a *yod*, must be written from memory, the scribe not having looked at the codex before him.... Between every consonant the space of a hair or thread must intervene; between every word the breadth of a narrow consonant; between every new *parashah*, or section, the breadth of nine consonants; between every book, three lines. The fifth book of Moses must terminate exactly with a line; but the rest need not do so. Besides this, the copyist must sit in full Jewish dress, wash his whole body, not begin to write the name of God with a pen newly dipped in ink, and should a king address him while writing that name he must take no notice of him.... The rolls in which these regulations are not observed are condemned to be buried in the ground or burned; or they are banished to the schools, to be used as reading-books."[1]

This strict set of regulations which governed the early Jewish scribes is a chief factor which guarantees the accurate transmission of the Old Testament text. There are also all the meticulous precautions observed by the Massoretes in their vigorous effort to detect scribal errors. Variations undoubtedly existed in the manuscripts used by the Massoretes, but they could not have been numerous. All available evidence on the question shows that the type of text made permanent by the Massoretes was extant in the centuries which antedate the coming of Christ.

The Dead Sea Scrolls

In March of 1948 the discovery of some ancient manuscripts found in the vicinity of the Dead Sea was first reported. An Arab boy, as the story goes, was looking for a lost goat and by chance stumbled on a cave. Inside the cave he found some jars containing several old leather rolls. These rolls eventually were sold and now are the prized treasure of the young state of Israel.

Since the first news of these scrolls, numerous others have been located in the same region. In all about 350 rolls, most of them fragmentary, have been uncovered. These scrolls were produced by a deeply religious community of Jews who had taken up their station in the desert "to prepare the way of the Lord." Many of the scrolls concern only the peculiar beliefs of the sect, yet there are many others which contain the text of fragmentary portions of the Old Testament. Actually fragments of almost every book of the Old Testament have turned up, and since less than half of the present materials have been deciphered others may be forthcoming.

The most important of these manuscripts are two scrolls of the book of Isaiah. One is complete, except for a few words, and is known as Isaiah A; the other one, known as Isaiah B, is not complete but contains a considerable portion of material (Isa. 41-59). The amazing story of these manuscripts is bound up with their age. Isaiah A dates back to 100 B.C. or earlier, while Isaiah

---

A column of the Isaiah Scroll of the Dead Sea Scrolls.
Courtesy of the American Schools of Oriental Research.

B is but a little later. Here are scrolls that are a thousand years earlier than the oldest of our previous Hebrew manuscripts!

What do these scrolls reveal about our text? How do they compare with the manuscripts of the Massoretic text from which they are separated by so many centuries? Do these newly discovered manuscripts demand such changes in the text that require also changes in our faith?

These scrolls tell us much, but chiefly that there has scarcely been, at least since the first or second centuries B.C., a major change in the form of the Hebrew text. As Professor F. F. Bruce expresses it, "The new evidence confirms what we had already good reason to believe — that the Jewish scribes of the early Christian centuries copied and recopied the text of the Hebrew Bible with the utmost fidelity."[2]

The exactness of this statement can be illustrated in various ways. The Isaiah A scroll became known in time for the Revised Standard Version of 1952 to take its text into account. With the complete scroll of Isaiah A at hand, the revision committee adopted only thirteen variant readings attested by Isaiah A in contrast with the Massoretic text. And of these thirteen, Millar Burrows, a member of the translating committee and from the beginning a first-rank authority on the scrolls, later confessed that he personally felt that some of these departures from the Massoretic text were a mistake.[3] The reader of the Revised Standard Version can locate these passages for himself by checking the footnote citation, "One ancient MS." The one ancient manuscript referred to is Isaiah A of the Dead Sea Scrolls.

Some of the changes made in the Revised Standard translation, however, are distinct improvements. A good illustration appears in Isaiah 21:8. The Revised Standard reads: "Then he who saw cried." Isaiah A has the reading "he who saw," while the Massoretic text reads "a lion." The meanings in the two texts are quite different, but the two Hebrew words underlying the expressions are very similar in appearance and could be easily

---

[2]F. F. Bruce, *Second Thoughts on the Dead Sea Scrolls* (Grand Rapids: Wm. B. Eerdmans Publishing Company, 1956), pp. 61-62.

[3]Millar Burrows, *The Dead Sea Scrolls* (New York: The Viking Press, 1955), p. 305.

confused. In the context the translation of the Revised Standard Version, as compared with the King James and American Standard Versions, makes much better sense. We are fortunate that the Isaiah Scroll has preserved this good reading.

As a whole the texts of these ancient scrolls are remarkably like our text today. The sixth chapter of Isaiah, chosen at random, may be taken as an example. Comparing Isaiah A and our present Hebrew text we are able to count thirty-seven variant readings in this chapter. But practically all of these variants are no more than spelling differences. Only three of them are large enough to be reflected in an English translation, and of these not a one is significant. These three variants are: "they were calling" instead of "one called to another" (vs. 3) ; "holy, holy" instead of "holy, holy, holy" (vs. 3) ; and "sins" for "sin" (vs. 7) . In these cases our present text is unquestionably better than that found in Isaiah A. What differences exist in the text, in the overwhelming majority of the cases are very trivial in nature. This has prompted Millar Burrows to say: "It is a matter for wonder that through something like a thousand years the text underwent so little alteration. As I said in my first article on the scroll, 'Herein lies its chief importance, supporting the fidelity of the Massoretic tradition.' "[4]

Summary

Our oldest Hebrew manuscripts date no farther back than the ninth century. This might prove to be a difficult barrier for the Old Testament text were it not for the safeguards devised and followed by the Massoretes and the strict rules observed by earlier Jewish scribes. Early versions of the Old Testament and other sources are of great value since they attest to the reliability of our present text. The Biblical documents of the Dead Sea Scrolls are nothing short of sensational. The most important are the two Isaiah scrolls which, although they exhibit many minor differences, confirm beyond doubt the accuracy of our present Hebrew text.

---

[4]*Ibid.,* p. 304.

For Consideration

1. Contrast the ages of the earliest Old and New Testament manuscripts. What accounts for the difference of age between them?
2. Who were the Massoretes? What did they do to secure the proper pronunciation of the Hebrew text?
3. List some of the devices used by the Massoretes to safeguard the accurate transmission of the text.
4. What are some of the regulations which governed the preparation of copies of the Pentateuch for Synagogue use?
5. Name some of the other materials on the Old Testament text. Which of these are the most important?
6. What are the most important documents of the Dead Sea Scrolls? How does their age compare to the age of previous Hebrew manuscripts?
7. Discuss the accuracy of our Hebrew text today in relation to the Dead Sea Scrolls. Do these amazing materials confirm the reliability of our accepted Old Testament text?

9

The Canon of the Scriptures

Most of the preceding study has been given to the transmission of the Bible text — how and under what conditions the text has come down to us, and how we can be sure that we have the exact words of this text. It is now time to take up another phase of the history of the Bible: the collection of books which comprise *Scripture*. Many religious books were written during the period of the Old and New Testaments. Which of these books rightfully belongs to the Bible, and which should be excluded from it? On what grounds are some writings to be accepted as Scripture and others to be rejected? The answers to these questions can be found in the study of what is known as the *canon* of the Scriptures.

The English word *canon* goes back to the Greek word *kanon* and then to the Hebrew *qaneh.* Its basic meaning is *reed,* our English word *cane* being derived from it. Since a reed was sometimes used as a measuring rod, the word *kanon* came to mean a standard or rule. It was also used to refer to a list or index, and when so applied to the Bible denotes the list of books which are received as Holy Scripture. Thus if one speaks of the *canonical* writings, he is speaking of those books which are regarded as having divine authority and which comprise our Bible.

There is a difference between the canonicity of a book and the authority of that book. A book's canonicity depends upon its authority. When Paul, for example, writes to the Corinthians, his letter is to be acknowledged as possessing divine authority (I Cor. 14:37). This letter had authority from the moment he wrote it, yet it could not be referred to as canonical until it was received in a list of accepted writings formed sometime later. At a later time it was accepted as canonical because of its inherent authority. A book first has divine authority based on its inspiration, and then attains canonicity due to its general acceptance as a divine product. No church council by its decrees can *make* the books of the Bible authoritative. The books of the Bible possess their own authority and indeed had this authority long before there were any councils of the church. The teachings of the Roman Catholic Church completely ignore this important point.

The Canon of the Old Testament

Good evidence exists in the New Testament which shows that by the time of Jesus the canon of the Old Covenant had been fixed. It cannot be questioned that Jesus and his apostles time after time quote from a body of writings as "Scripture." If some writings were "Scripture," others were not. Some writings were canonical and others were non-canonical.

The canonical writings, according to Jesus, are composed of the Law of Moses, the Prophets, and the Psalms (Luke 24:44). This threefold division is undoubtedly equivalent to the three divisions of the Hebrew Scriptures — the Law, the Prophets, and the Writings (cf. Chapter 2). Jesus also gives some indication concerning the books included in the Old Testament canon. He once spoke of the time "from the blood of Abel to the blood of Zachariah, who perished between the altar and the sanctuary" (Luke 11:51), thus referring to the martyrs of the Old Testament. The first martyr of the Old Testament, of course, was Abel and the last martyr was Zachariah (cf. II Chron. 24:20-21). It is to be kept in mind that the Jewish order of the Old Testament differs from ours, and that Chronicles is placed at the end of the Hebrew Bible. Thus the Old Testament which Jesus knew was a collection of writings reaching from Genesis to Chronicles, with all of the other books in between, a collection which embraces the same books found in our Old Testament today. When toward the close of the first century Jewish leaders at Jamnia (located near the coast of Palestine) specified these books as being the authoritative Scriptures, they were but confirming what for some- time had been recognized as the canon of the Old Testament.

Additional evidence which applies here comes from Josephus, a well-known Jewish writer of the first century, and from early Christian writers such as Origen and Jerome. Josephus clearly speaks concerning the number of books received as "Scripture" by the Jews. "We have not 10,000 books among us, disagreeing with and contradicting one another, but only twenty-two books which contain the records of all time, and are justly believed to be divine. Five of these are by Moses, and contain his laws and traditions of the origin of mankind until his death. . . . From the death of Moses till the reign of Artaxerxes, king of Persia, who reigned after Xerxes, the prophets who succeeded Moses wrote down what happened in their times in thirteen books; and the remaining four books contain hymns to God and precepts for the conduct of human life."[1] It is the opinion of most scholars that Josephus in deriving his number of twenty-two books joined Ruth to Judges and Lamentations to Jeremiah; and remembering that the Jews enumerated their books differently, that the twelve minor prophets were considered as one book and that others, like I and II Samuel, I and II Kings, I and II Chronicles and Ezra-Nehemiah were likewise counted as one book each, the twenty-two books mentioned by Josephus equal our present thirty-nine books.

In the third century A.D., Origen confirms the testimony of Josephus on the twenty-two books of the Old Testament. Giving both their Hebrew and Greek titles, he lists them as follows: (1-5) the Five Books of Moses, (6) Joshua, (7) Judges-Ruth, (8) I and II Samuel, (9) I and II Kings, (10) Chronicles, (11) Ezra-Nehemiah, (12) Psalms, (13) Proverbs, (14) Ecclesiastes, (15) Song of Solomon, (16) Isaiah, (17) Jeremiah-Lamentations, (18) Daniel, (19) Ezekiel, (20) Job, and (21) Esther.[2] Origen omits from his list the Book of the Twelve (the minor prophets), but this is clearly an accidental omission since it is necessary to make up his own number of twenty-two. A little later other Christian writers, including the scholarly Jerome, point to these same books as the canonical materials for the Old Testament.

The Canon of the New Testament

About the middle of the second century a Christian writer, Justin Martyr, stated that on Sundays in the Christian worship assemblies the "memoirs of the apostles" were read together with

---

1Josephus, *Against Apion* I. 8.
2Cited by Eusebius, *Ecclesiastical History* VI. 25.

the "writings of the prophets."[3] It is evident, then, that not long after the close of the apostolic age the New Testament writings were being read generally among the churches. What brought this about? How was it possible that within a short time the writings of the apostles were being used for public reading as well as the writings of the Old Testament prophets?

When the church of Christ was first established it had no thought of a New Testament. Its Bible was the Old Testament and its new teachings were based on the authority of Christ as personally mediated through the apostles. Soon inspired men came to put in writing divine regulations directed both to churches and individuals. It was inevitable that these regulations would become normative, for Christians could not have less respect for them than for their Christ. Thus Paul's letters were carefully gathered into a single whole; next came a collection of the Four Gospels, and then all the others followed. Because these collections were made at different times and places, the contents of the various collections were not always the same. This helps to explain why not all of the New Testament books were at first received without hesitation; while in other instances uncertainty of a book's authorship, as in the case of Hebrews, presented temporary obstacles to universal acceptance. This was the exception, however, rather than the rule; and gradually each book on its own merit — not without, Christians believe, a guiding Providence — took its place in the accepted canon of New Testament Scripture.

If it is no later than the middle of the second century when the apostles' letters became widely read in public meetings, it is no later than the last half of that century when substantial lists of the New Testament books appear. An example of one of these lists from this time is known as the Muratorian Fragment. Its name is derived from L. A. Muratori, who first discovered the list and published it in the eighteenth century. Part of this early list of the New Testament books has been lost. The Gospel of Luke is the first mentioned by name, but it is referred to as the "third" Gospel, indicating that Matthew and Mark were at the head of the list; then follow John, Acts, thirteen letters of Paul and

---

[3] Justin Martyr, *First Apology*, Chap. 67.

others. The only books not included in the list are Hebrews, James, I and II Peter and I John, and were it not for a text seemingly derived from a mutilated copy the list undoubtedly would be more complete. On any other assumption it is difficult to account for the omissions, especially those of I Peter and I John. Notwithstanding these omissions this early list provides in broad outline the substance of our modern New Testament.

In the third century Origen names all of the New Testament books, but says that Hebrews, James, II and III John, and Jude were questioned by some.[4] Eusebius of the fourth century likewise names all of the New Testament books.[5] He says, however, that some books (James, II Peter, II and III John, and Jude) were suspected, but that they were accepted by the majority. In 367 A.D. Athanasius of Alexandria published a list of 27 New Testament books which were accepted in his time, and these are the same twenty-seven which are recognized today. The Bible had grown in relative proportion to its divine revelation — gradually — and its books likewise had gradually assumed the roles which their inherent authority demanded.

Related Observations

It is sometimes said that the line of demarcation between the New Testament books and other Christian writings was not always clear, that the early church scarcely made distinction between the two. But there is little evidence to support this charge. There were indeed a number of good books which were circulating among Christians of that day, written by uninspired men. Especially important among these are the Epistle of Barnabas and the Shepherd of Hermas. The first was written toward the close of the apostolic age by some one other than the New Testament Barnabas; the second is an allegory which dates back to the first half of the second century and was written by a member of the church at Rome called Hermas. Yet these books were never above suspicion, nor were they ever received on a par with the genuine apostolic writings. In the case of the Shepherd of Hermas, for example, the above mentioned Muratorian Fragment

---

4Cited by Eusebius, *Ecclesiastical History* VI. 25.
5Eusebius, *Ecclesiastical History* III. 25.

states that it could be read in public worship but that it was not to be counted among the prophetic or apostolic writings.

The restriction concerning the Shepherd of Hermas serves to illustrate the significant principle that some books could be read for edification in public worship which were not at the time regarded as possessing divine authority. In this category fall such writings as the Shepherd of Hermas and the Epistle of Barnabas. These and a few others were sometimes included in the early manuscripts, but according to the Muratorian Fragment it is a mistake to think that every book which was read in the churches was necessarily accorded apostolic standing. Even today in public assemblies, as purposes of teaching and edification may demand, selections from secular works are sometimes read. It was no different in the days of the early church, nor is there sufficient reason to think that they were less discerning in distinguishing between inspired and non-inspired materials.

Summary

The word *canon* as used in this study refers to the list of books which are acknowledged as being divinely inspired and are included in the Bible. The formation of the canon was a gradual process, just as the books themselves came into being gradually. By the time of our Lord it is evident that the Old Testament canon was well-defined: a clear distinction is maintained between "Scripture" and non-Scripture. Evidence as to the exact books of Old Testament Scripture is furnished by the numerous quotations found in the New Testament of the Old Testament and from other early Christian and non-Christian sources. As to the New Testament books, not long after they were written they were being read regularly in the church assemblies. They were held in high esteem by early Christians — the words of Jesus and His apostles could not be less authoritative than the Scriptures of the Old Testament. In this way the New Testament canon gradually took shape; so that within a century or two the New Testament books as they are known today had been collected and constituted the supreme authority for the primitive church.

In conclusion, it is necessary to emphasize that no church through its councils *made* the canon of Scripture. No church — in particular the Roman Catholic Church — by its decrees gave to or pronounced upon the books of the Bible their infallibility. The Bible owes its authority to no individual or group. The church does not control the canon, but the canon controls the church. Although divine authority was attributed to the New Testament books by the later church, this authority was not derived from the church but was inherent in the books themselves. As a child identifies its mother, the later church *identified* the books which it regarded as having unique authority.

For Consideration

1. What is meant by the *canon* of the Scriptures? What familiar English word is related to the word *canon?*
2. Distinguish between a book's canonicity and its authority. Is authority dependent on canonicity or canonicity dependent on authority?
3. Is there any information in the New Testament which has bearing on the Old Testament canon? What statement of Jesus indicates which books were included in the Old Testament of his day? Did His Old Testament differ from ours?
4. List other evidences on the Old Testament canon. How is it that the twenty-two books of the Jews equal our thirty-nine books?
5. Describe briefly the first stages in the formation of a New Testament canon.
6. Name some of the early lists of New Testament books. Is it natural to expect some differences in the early lists? Why?
7. Explain why a decision of a church council cannot make certain books infallible. Does the church control the canon of Scripture?

10

The Apocryphal Books

Today there is very little discussion concerning which books rightfully belong in the Bible. The canon of the Holy Scriptures is settled. But the question of the canon has been decided differently in the general parts of Christendom. Catholicism and Protestantism are united in their acceptance of the twenty-seven books of the New Testament, but concerning the books of the Old Testament there is not this agreement. When one picks up a copy of a Catholic Bible he sees that there are several additional books included in its Old Testament section which are not found in Protestant Bibles. These extra books are generally known as the *apocrypha*.

The word *apocrypha* has come into the English language from the Greek and basically means *hidden*. It was used very early in the sense of *secretive* or *concealed,* but was also used in reference to a book whose origin was doubtful or unknown. Eventually the word took on the meaning of *non-canonical,* and thus for centuries the non-canonical books have been known as *apocryphal* books. Yet in Protestant circles "the apocrypha" is the normal designation for those extra books which are found in the Catholic Old Testament. In a stricter sense, however, these books might be better termed "the Old Testament apocrypha," since there are New Testament apocryphal writings as well.

Apocryphal Books of the Old Testament

The Old Testament Apocrypha include either fourteen or fifteen books, depending on the method of counting, which were written in the period of 200 B.C. to 100 A.D. The most convenient and readable edition of the aprocrypha has been put out by Thomas Nelson and Sons in a special edition of the Revised

Standard Version (1957). The titles and order of books in this edition are as follows:

1. The First Book of Esdras (also known as Third Esdras)
2. The Second Book of Esdras (also known as Fourth Esdras)
3. Tobit
4. Judith
5. The Additions to the Book of Esther
6. The Wisdom of Solomon
7. Ecclesiasticus, or the Wisdom of Jesus the Son of Sirach
8. Baruch
9. The Letter of Jeremiah (This letter is sometimes incorporated as the last chapter of Baruch. When this is done the number of books is fourteen instead of fifteen.)
10. The Prayer of Azariah and the Song of the Three Young Men
11. Susanna
12. Bel and the Dragon
13. The Prayer of Manasseh
14. The First Book of Maccabees
15. The Second Book of Maccabees

Three of these fifteen books (I and II Esdras and the Prayer of Manasseh) are not considered canonical by the Roman Catholic Church. In Catholic Bibles the remaining twelve are interspersed among and attached to the undisputed thirty-nine books of the Old Testament: Tobit, Judith, Wisdom of Solomon, Ecclesiasticus, Baruch with the letter of Jeremiah, and I and II Maccabees which are arranged separately; the Additions to Esther are joined to Esther; and appended to the book of Daniel are the Prayer of Azariah and the Song of the Three Young Men (added after Dan. 3:23), and Susanna, and Bel and the Dragon. (I and II Esdras of the Catholic Bible are not the same as the I and II Esdras in the above list, but are different designations for our books Ezra and Nehemiah.) Since several of the apocryphal writings are combined with canonical books, the Catholic Bible numbers altogether forty-six books in its Old Testament. Non-Catholic editions of the English Bible since 1535, including early editions of the familiar King James Version, separate these apocryphal books from the canonical Old Testament.

Contents of These Books

The Old Testament Apocrypha covers a broad range of subjects and represents different varieties of literary form. For purposes of convenience they may be classified under the following division:

1. Historical — I Esdras, I and II Maccabees.
2. Legendary — Tobit, Judith, Additions to Esther, Additions to Daniel (Prayer of Azariah and Song of the Three Young Men, Susanna, and Bel and the Dragon).
3. Prophetic — Baruch, Letter of Jeremiah, Prayer of Manasseh, II Esdras.
4. Ethical — Ecclesiasticus, Wisdom of Solomon.

Something of the character of these writings will now be mentioned.

1. Historical. I Esdras is an ill-arranged collection of much of the material found in the canonical Ezra (Esdras is a Greek form for Ezra), and includes also worthless and legendary accounts which are not supported by the books of Ezra, Nehemiah and II Chronicles. It is also known as the "Greek Ezra" in contrast to the "Hebrew Ezra" (the Canonical Ezra). I Maccabees is an important source of information on Jewish history during the second century B.C. The book derives its name from Maccabeus, the surname of the Judas who led the Jews in revolt against Syrian oppression. It was written probably during the early part of the first century B.C. II Maccabees concerns the same general period, but is not as historically reliable as I Maccabees.

2. Legendary. The Book of Tobit was written about 200 B.C. It tells the story of a religious Israelite named Tobit who was carried as a captive to Nineveh by the Assyrians. Its purpose is to encourage the keeping of the Law, yet the ficticious character of its tales detracts from its usefulness. The book of Judith is likewise to be classified as fiction. Judith is the name of a Jewish widow who successfully charms and kills the leader of an enemy army, thus delivering her city and people from impending destruction. This story of heroism was most likely composed during the time of the Maccabean revolt in order to incite courage and patriotism against the Syrian foe.

The Additions to Esther are expansions of the canonical Esther which were probably handed down through the centuries by oral tradition. The Additions to Daniel contain folk-tales and legends which could not have originated much earlier than 100 B.C. and form no part of the genuine text of Daniel.

3. Prophetic. Baruch purports to come from the hand of Jeremiah's friend of that name. The contents of the book not only make this claim impossible, but help to fix the real date of composition at some point after 70 A.D. The letter of Jeremiah, which for no good reason is often appended to Baruch, is a brief notation on the vanities of idolatry. The Prayer of Manasseh, written perhaps in the second century B.C., is a prayer put in the mouth of King Manasseh after he was taken captive to Babylon. II Esdras is a collection of materials written at different times (from c. 100 B.C. to c. 200 A.D.). It is of such inferior quality that it is unquestionably non-canonical.

4. Ethical. Ecclesiasticus, or the Wisdom of Jesus the Son of Sirach, is one of the chief works of the Apocrypha. It was written by a Palestinian Jew about 200 B.C. in a style similar to the wise sayings of the Book of Proverbs. The Wisdom of Solomon is a book of ancient Jewish philosophy. It is evidently to be traced back to the city of Alexandria and to the first century A.D.

Why These Books Rejected

A brief survey of these books has indicated something of what they are like. Some of the books of the Apocrypha, such as I Maccabees and Ecclesiasticus, are truly worth while. The question, however, concerns not their usefulness but their place in relation to the authoritative Scriptures. Should they be received as "Scripture" or rejected? And if they are to be rejected, on what grounds? Are there really good reasons why they should not be accepted as divinely authoritative?

There are many valid reasons why the Apocrypha cannot bear acceptance as "Holy Scripture."

1. These books were never included in the Hebrew canon of the Old Testament. Josephus, it will be recalled, expressly limited the Hebrew canon to twenty-two books, which are the exact equivalent of the thirty-nine books of our Old Testament. Josephus knew of other Jewish writings down to his time, but he did not regard them as having equal authority with the

canonical works.[1] So the Apocrypha were never received by the Jews as God-given Scripture. This takes on its full significance when it is remembered that the Old Testament is a Jewish collection of Jewish history and law — and there is no evidence that these books were ever accepted by any Jewish community, either in or outside of the land of Palestine.

2. These books, as far as the evidence goes, were never accepted as canonical by Jesus and His apostles. In the previous chapter it was learned that the Old Testament which Jesus knew is our Old Testament today. Jesus' Old Testament was the Hebrew Old Testament, and the Hebrew Old Testament has never numbered these apocryphal writings. The apostles in their preaching mention many Old Testament events, but they never refer to any incidents or characters of the Apocrypha. The New Testament writers quote from practically all of the Old Testament books, but nowhere quote from the Apocrypha as "Scripture." The canon of the Old Testament accepted by Jesus and His apostles should be sufficient for the Christian today.

3. These books were not accepted as Scripture by such Jewish writers of the first century as Philo and Josephus; the Jewish council at Jamnia (c. 90 A.D.); and by such eminent Christian writers as Origen and Jerome. About 400 A.D. the great Christian scholar Jerome, whose translation of the Latin Vulgate remains the basis of the official Roman Catholic Bible, strongly maintained that these books were "apocryphal" and were not to be included in the canon of Scripture.

4. These books do not evidence intrinsic qualities of inspiration. Great portions of these books are obviously legendary and fictitious. Often they contain historical, chronological and geographical errors. In Judith, for example, Holofernes is described as being the general of "Nebuchadnezzar who ruled over the Assyrians in the great city of Ninevah" (1:1). Actually Holofernes was a Persian general, and, of course, Nebuchadnezzar was king of the Babylonians in Babylon. Some of these books contradict themselves and contradict the canonical Scriptures. It is said in Baruch that God hears the prayers of the dead (3:4).

---

[1]Josephus, *Against Apion* I. 8.

5. These books have been shrouded with continual uncertainty. Since they were not regarded as authoritative by the Jews, they had to gain their recognition elsewhere. This recognition came from some segments of the Greek-speaking church, with the result that eventually these books became incorporated into the Greek and Latin Bibles. But there is no evidence that the Septuagint (the Greek translation of the Old Testament) ever had a fixed or closed canon of books. No two early Greek manuscripts agree as to which books are to be included in the Septuagint, and not all of those included in the Septuagint are accepted even by the Roman Catholic Church. The Septuagint itself is a witness against one book of the Apocrypha (II Esdras) since it is found in no manuscript of the Septuagint.

6. These books cannot be maintained on a compromise basis. The Church of England gives to the Apocrypha a semi-canonical status: they may be read in public worship "for example of life and instruction of manners" but not in order "to establish any doctrine." This position assumes that the Apocrypha at times may add to or conflict with the established teachings of the canonical Scriptures. If this is true, then the Apocrypha should not be read in public worship, for what is read regularly in public worship tends to be authoritative for the congregation. To allow the Apocrypha to be read in public worship is a strange way to show their inferior rank.

7. Objections to these books cannot be overruled by dictatorial authority. On April 8, 1546, in the Fourth Session of the Council of Trent, the Roman Catholic Church pronounced the Old Testament Apocrypha (except I and II Esdras and the Prayer of Manasseh) as authoritative and canonical Scripture. This was done even though in different periods of its own history officials of the Roman Church had been out-spoken against the Apocrypha as Scripture. But this action was not unnatural for a religious body whose whole structure is framed according to traditions and whose faith is derived equally as much from the "fathers" and "popes" as from the Scriptures. It appears that the Apocrypha would never have posed a serious problem were it not for the usurped power of Rome over Scripture. Yet Rome with all of its "infallibility" cannot make the fallible Apocrypha infallible.

The Apocryphal Books of the New Testament

The Old Testament Apocrypha is usually thought of when one mentions the apocryphal books. Nevertheless there are other apocryphal writings, many of which are known as the New Testament Apocrypha. The New Testament Apocrypha include a variety of literary types: Gospels, Acts, Epistles and Apocalypses. These were written under assumed names of the apostles and others during the second century and later. They contain fanciful stories about Jesus and the apostles. The Apocryphal Gospels often deal with the early years of Jesus and portray him as a temperamental child, here causing the death of some of his playmates and there giving life to a dried fish. The Apocryphal Acts and others indulge in similar nonsense.

The writings of the Apostolic Fathers (80-180 A.D.) are not to be classified as New Testament Apocrypha. They are simply letters of edification and encouragement written by ordinary Christians; they do not profess apostolic wisdom and authority. These writings, along with the apocryphal books, are sometimes erroneously described as "the lost books of the Bible," a sensational and misleading title because these books were never a part of the Bible.

Summary

The word *apocrypha* may be used with equal application to the non-canonical books of the Old and New Testaments. Generally speaking, however, it is a common designation for a special group of fourteen or fifteen books, most of which are included in the Old Testament of the Roman Catholic Bible. The Apocrypha may be divided into four groups: (1) historical, (2) legendary, (3) prophetic and (4) ethical. These books are useful but are not to be regarded as Scripture for the following reasons:

1. They were never included in the Hebrew Old Testament.
2. They were never accepted as canonical by Jesus and His Apostles.
3. They were not accepted by early Jewish and Christian writers.
4. They do not evidence intrinsic qualities of inspiration.
5. They have been shrouded with continual uncertainty.

6. They cannot be maintained on a compromise basis.
7. Objections to them cannot be overruled by dictatorial authority.

The apocryphal books are rightfully rejected from our Bible.

FOR CONSIDERATION

1. What is the basic meaning of the word *apocrypha?* How is it generally used?
2. Recite in order the books of the Apocrypha. How many are there? Which two books are sometimes joined together and thus affect the total number of books?
3. List the alternative names of the following books: I Esdras, II Esdras, Ecclesiasticus, and the "Greek Ezra."
4. As to subject-matter, how may the books of the Apocrypha be divided?
5. What three books of the Apocrypha are not included in the Roman Catholic Bible?
6. Discuss some of the values of the Apocrypha.
7. List seven reasons why the Apocrypha should not be received as Scripture. Discuss each one of these reasons. Is each a valid reason?

11

The English Bible to 1611

Another phase of the Bible's transmission lies in the history of English translations. Christianity made its entrance into Britain no later than the fourth century, but at that time the Scriptures were not available to the people in translation. The Latin language was then assuming dominance in the West as the language of the learned, which meant that the early Bibles in England were not in English but Latin. Yet it was in England, so long deprived of the living Word, where the battle was fought and won for the right of the common man to have his Bible in his own language.

The Earliest English Versions

The beginnings of the English Bible go back to the middle of the seventh century. An unlearned laborer by the name of Caedmon is reported to have arranged in verse form stories of the Bible on subjects ranging from the creation to the work of the apostles. Although these verses were not really translations, they mark the first known attempt to put the Bible accounts in the native Anglo-Saxon. The next generation saw the first actual translation of any part of the Bible in English. The translation was the work of Aldhelm (d. 709), and the portion of Scripture translated was the book of Psalms. A little later the venerable Bede (d. 735) is said to have finished in the last hours of his life a translation of the Gospel of John, but of his translation nothing has been preserved. Toward the close of the ninth century King Alfred (d. 901) led his people in a religious reform that resulted in a translation of the Psalms and other sections of Scripture. In the tenth century Abbot Aelfric translated additional portions of the Old Testament. Altogether the Old English versions that have survived include the Pentateuch, some historical books of the Old Testament, the Psalms and the Gospels.

The Norman conquest in 1066 brought about many changes in England. Chief among these was a modification of the language, now known as Middle English. It was not until the thirteenth and fourteenth centuries before parts of the Bible were put in English, and here the names of William of Shoreham and Richard Rolle stand out. It was their work on the Psalms in the first half of the fourteenth century that planted the seed of a struggle which was to last for two centuries in putting the Bible in the hands of the common people.

Wycliffe and Tyndale

A memorable name in the story of the English Bible is John Wycliffe. The England that he knew most of his life (1330-1384) was full of faction and unrest, much of which had been brought on by the Roman Pope's excessive demands for money. Oxford scholar and teacher, Wycliffe in the controversy over Papal oppression emerged as the champion of the people. Wycliffe's first written work was in defense of Parliament in 1366 for its refusal to turn over money claimed by the Pope; and it was this uncompromising spirit that shortly afterward urged him on in the fight for social and religious reforms. So Wycliffe and his associates called England to the great spiritual revival of the fourteenth century.

Wycliffe had the peculiar idea that the common man was worth something. "No man," he said, "was so rude a scholar but that he might learn the words of the Gospel according to his simplicity." In this belief, during the last years of his life and with the assistance of some of his students, Wycliffe undertook a translation of the Scriptures from the Latin into the English tongue. This work was completed about 1382, the first translation to be made in English of the complete Bible. It is not known how much of the translation was made by Wycliffe personally, perhaps the New Testament and a part of the Old Testament. Yet it is correct to describe it as the Wycliffe version, for it was due to his scholarship and under his guidance that the historic project was accomplished. In 1388 John Purvey, a close friend and associate, thoroughly corrected and revised

Wycliffe's first version, and it was Purvey's revised Bible that held sway until the sixteenth century.

The true father of the English Bible is William Tyndale. The story of Tyndale and his unrelenting efforts to put the Bible in the hands of the people is a story of triumph mingled with tears. In the year of 1509 the monk-scholar Erasmus came to Cambridge as professor of Greek. The following year young Tyndale also came to Cambridge, perhaps to study Greek under Erasmus. Under the influence of his training received at Cambridge, and earlier at Oxford, Tyndale formed the ambition which was to be his chief aim in life — to give to the English people a translation of the Bible based not on Latin but upon the original Greek and Hebrew. He once said to one of his opponents: "If God spare my life, ere many years I will cause a boy that driveth the plow shall know more of the Scripture than thou doest." Consciously or unconsciously he was reflecting a similar conviction of Erasmus: "I would to God the plowman would sing a text of the scripture at his plow, and the weaver at his loom with this would drive away the tediousness of time. I would that the wayfaring man with this pastime would expel the weariness of his journey."

Erasmus had issued in 1516 the first printed New Testament in Greek, and Tyndale had set out to translate it. In 1524 Tyndale had to leave England, after finding out, he said, "that there was no place to do it [translate the New Testament] in all of England." At Hamburg in the following year his translation was completed, and at Cologne he sought to have it printed. By now Tyndale's efforts of translation had identified him with the Reformer Martin Luther, who had recently finished a translation in German. So the many enemies of the new Reformation and of Luther were likewise the enemies of Tyndale. Accordingly, Tyndale had to flee from Cologne with the sheets of his partially printed New Testament. At Worms, which was disposed favorably to the Reformation, the printing of his New Testament was completed. Early in 1526 the first copies were smuggled into England and bought with enthusiasm. Officials of the Church spoke out in condemnation of the translation; copies were obtained and burned in public ceremony; money was subscribed to buy up incoming copies. But all concentrated opposition could not wipe out a movement which was making itself felt around the world.

In the meantime Tyndale had taken up his work of translating the Old Testament from Hebrew. By 1530 he had translated and published the Pentateuch; then followed Jonah (1531), a revised Genesis (1534), and two additional editions of his New Testament (1534-35). By now his translations, although not welcomed as yet, were not so violently opposed by official England; and it appeared as though the long-fought contest might turn in his favor. But many Romanists were still determined to stamp out heresy. Tyndale was thus betrayed and imprisoned in 1534. In 1536, after spending months in prison, he was strangled and burned at the stake, crying, "Lord, open the King of England's eyes."

Other Sixteenth Century Translations

Tyndale died, but "he had lighted such a candle, by God's grace, in England, as should never be put out."[1] Even before his death the tide had begun to change. We like to think that Tyndale while in prison had heard of the publication in England (1535) of a Bible partly based on his own. This Bible was that of Miles Coverdale, a former friend and associate of Tyndale. Coverdale was not the scholar that Tyndale was, but his translation is significant because it was the first in England to circulate without official hindrance.

A flood of translations and revisions was to follow. Matthew's Bible, actually the work of Tyndale's friend John Rogers, appeared in 1537. It was a combined edition of both Tyndale and Coverdale. Taverner's Bible of 1539 was an independent revision of Matthew's Bible, and its chief contribution has to do with a number of improved renderings in the New Testament.

In the same year another revision of Matthew's Bible came out, known as the Great Bible. Edited by Coverdale, it was the first of the English Bibles authorized to be read in the churches. It was the wish of Henry VIII that it go abroad among the people, and in keeping with the king's wish a copy of the Great

---

[1]Sir Frederic Kenyon, *Our Bible and the Ancient Manuscripts*. Revised by A. W. Adams. (New York: Harper and Brothers, 1958), p. 290.

Bible was placed in every church in the land. People flocked eagerly to the churches to see the Bibles which had been set up for reading, and at times the preachers complained because the people chose rather to read the Bible than listen to their sermons. Tyndale's dying prayer at last had been answered: the Lord had opened the king of England's eyes.

Another Bible, however, was destined to be the most popular Bible of the century. It was the Geneva Bible of 1560, so called because it was printed in Geneva. Being produced in legible type, in small form, with accompanying commentary and illustrations, it became the Bible for the family as the Great Bible was the Bible for the church. It was the first translation to print each verse as a paragraph and to put words in italics not represented in the original texts. It is sometimes known as the "Breeches Bible" because it says that Adam and Eve "sewed figge tree leaves together, and made themselves breeches" (Gen. 3:7). The Geneva Bible was the Bible of Shakespeare and of the Pilgrims who journeyed to America.

But the Geneva Bible was not popular with the English Church officials. Its commentary presented the views of John Calvin and of the Reformation. A revision of the Great Bible was therefore begun by the English clergy, and when completed in 1568 was known as the Bishops' Bible. Four years later a second edition appeared, but the Bishops' Bible neither measured up to the scholarship nor attained to the popularity of the Geneva Bible.

The zeal of Protestant revisions and editions eventually forced into being a Roman Catholic translation of the Bible. An edition of the New Testament was produced in 1582 at the English college of Rheims; and in 1609-10 the college at Douai issued a translation of the Old Testament. The Rheims-Douai translation was thus the first Roman Catholic edition of the English Bible. It was translated, however, not from the original languages of Scripture, but on the basis of the Latin Vulgate.

The King James Version

It remained for the Authorized Version of 1611, better known as the King James Version, to do what its many predecessors had been unable to do — provide a translation for public and private use which was satisfactory to all. King James had summoned in 1604 a meeting of representatives of diverse religious groups to discuss the question of religious toleration. At this gathering, known as the Hampton Court Conference, Dr. John Reynolds of Oxford raised the possibility of a new translation. The king welcomed the suggestion and soon was working out the necessary procedures for its realization. James himself, it seems, laid down the main requirements which were to be followed, one of the chief rules being that there were to be no notes of comment except what was essential in translating the text. The Geneva Bible had been distinctively one-sided in its comments, and James knew that the way to satisfy all parties was to withhold from the margins the private viewpoint of any one party. Such provisions for the new translation were probably the wisest thing that the otherwise unwise king ever did.

In 1607 the work of the translators was formally begun. Their task was not to make a new translation but to revise the 1602 edition of the Bishops' Bible. About forty-eight choice Greek and Hebrew scholars were selected and divided into six working companies, two at Westminster, two at Oxford and two at Cambridge. Each company, restricted in its labors by detailed instructions, was assigned selected books to be translated; and the work of each company was sent to and reviewed by the other companies, appointed delegates of each company smoothing out the difficult spots. In this way the translation was the product of no individual or group but of the revisers as a whole.

The work of revision continued for two years and nine months, after which it was turned over to the printers. It was in 1611, seven years after the convening of the Hampton Court Conference, when the first copies of the new version came from the press. It was dedicated to the king, and on its title page were the words "Appointed to read in Churches." Accompanying it was a truly great preface entitled "The Translators to the Reader," in which the translators sought to justify their efforts against the many voices of critics who felt that their old Bibles were good enough. It is a pity that this preface, which is not to be confused with the dedication note, is no longer printed in many editions of the King James Bible. It is timely even today, and especially so for those who are always opposing new translations.

The King James translation has passed through many editions and has been modernized considerably during the course of years. In 1613 a new edition was issued which contained more than 400 variations from the original printing. Countless other emendations have taken place in the more than three centuries of its existence, so many changes indeed that the King James reader of today would be startled by the appearance of a 1611 edition.

Appointed for use in public worship, the King James immediately displaced the Bishops' Bible in the churches; but in private use the new translation received stiff competition from the popular Geneva Bible. Within a few decades, however, it had established itself as *the* translation for English-speaking people around the world. Reasons for its supremacy are not hard to find. First, Greek and Hebrew scholarship had made tremendous strides during the seventy-five years which had elapsed since the time of Tyndale. Study of the Biblical languages had ceased during the Middle Ages and had only recently been revived when Tyndale made his first translation. The sixteenth century following Tyndale was marked by such a resurgence of interest in the Biblical languages that when it came time for King James to constitute his revision committee he could look in many directions for men of capable and sound scholarship. Second, literary scholarship and learning in general at this time were at a high peak. It was the period of Elizabethan prose and poetry, the age in which Spenser and Shakespeare flowered. Under these influences the revisers were able to produce a translation carefully framed in a classic English style. Third, the revision was made at an opportune time. A good English translation was *needed,* and the translators were able to profit from both the excellencies and the shortcomings of previous translations. Fourth, the revision was the work of no one man or of no one party. England had been torn by religious factions, and partisan translations could not supply the remedy. A translation which endures can represent no single viewpoint, and that the King James Version has lasted for three and a half centuries is a tribute to its deliberate impartiality.

Summary

The story of the English Bible is as interesting as the story of a mighty nation. John Wycliffe was the first man to give to the English people a translation that could be read in their native tongue. Wycliffe's translation, however, was based on the Latin Vulgate. It was William Tyndale who was the first to envision and bring into reality an English translation based on the original Greek and Hebrew languages. Erasmus, who may have been his teacher at Cambridge, had greatly accelerated Tyndale's ambition by having recently published the New Testament in Greek. Tyndale's New Testament was first printed in 1525 and went through several editions, but Tyndale suffered martyrdom before he was able to complete his work on the Old Testament. Many translations followed Tyndale's: Coverdale's (1535), Matthew's Bible (1537), Taverner's (1539), the Great Bible (1539), the Geneva Bible (1560), the Bishops' Bible (1568), and the Authorized Version (1611). His translation was the first based on the Greek and Hebrew texts, and it was his labors which cleared the way for other translations. How appropriate it is that nine-tenths of Tyndale's translation is preserved today in the King James Version. William Tyndale is truly the father of the English Bible.

FOR CONSIDERATION

1. When did the Wycliffe translation first appear? Why was it so long before the English people had a translation in their own tongue?
2. Relate the high points in the story of Tyndale's translation of the New Testament. In what year did Tyndale finish his New Testament translation? Where was it printed and how did it get to England? Wycliffe's translation had been based on the Latin. Upon what did Tyndale base his translation?
3. List the translations (and the dates) which immediately followed Tyndale's. Which Bible was the first to be authorized for use in the churches?
4. Give several reasons which account for the popularity of the Geneva Bible. Contrast it with the Bishops' Bible of 1568.

5. Describe the events that led up to the appearance of the King James Bible. Was the King James Version a revision or a completely new translation? How many scholars were engaged in the work of translation? How long did they work?
6. List several concrete reasons for the supremacy of the King James Version over its predecessors.
7. Identify the following: a. John Purvey, b. Erasmus, c. Miles Coverdale, d. John Rogers, e. Rheims-Douai Version.

12

Recent Translations of the English Bible

The publication of the King James Version in 1611 was an epoch-making event in the history of the English Bible. Itself a revision, it was the climax of various translations and revisions. For many years it maintained an unquestioned supremacy, a supremacy so great that it has caused many people to regard it as the *final* word on Bible translation. But no translation is ever final. Because translators are human beings, there will always be room for improvements of translations. No translator can transcend his own time; he can only work in light of the knowledge of his day, with materials available to him, and put his translation in words spoken by his generation.

Weaknesses of the King James

It was inevitable that there would be revisions of the King James Bible. Several weaknesses of the King James made more recent revisions necessary:

1. The King James Version rests on an inadequate textual base. This is especially true with reference to the Greek text for the New Testament. The text underlying the King James was essentially a medieval text embodying a number of scribal mistakes that had accumulated through the years. Most of these textual variations were small in significance and did not affect materially the Bible message, but others were included which deserve no place in the Holy Scriptures. An example of this, as we have seen, is I John 5:7 (cf. Chapter 6). The revisers of 1611 are not at fault here. They simply did not have at their disposal the many manuscripts which are now known. It is important to

remember that four of the most valuable witnesses on the New Testament text (the Vatican, the Sinaitic, the Alexandrian, and the Ephraem Manuscripts) were not available when the King James translation was made. All of which means that the King James is a translation of an inferior Greek text, and therefore a revision of it based on earlier manuscripts was imperative.

2. The King James Version contains many archaic words whose meanings are either obscure or misleading. Some obsolete expressions are still intelligible, although they are extremely cumbersome and distracting to the reader: "howbeit," "holden," "peradventure," "aforetime," "because that," "for that," "thee," "thou," "thy," "thine," and many others. At other times, however, words are used which have drastically changed their meanings. In the seventeenth century "allege" was used for "prove," "communicate" for "share," "suffer" for "allow," "allow" for "approve," "let" for "hinder," "prevent" for "precede," "conversation" for "conduct," and so forth. These expressions are grossly misleading since they are still in use today but carry different associations.

Much of the grammar of the King James Version also is not in current usage. "Which" was characteristically employed for "who"; thus in Philippians 4:13 the King James reads: "I can do all things through Christ which strengtheneth me." Likewise "his" was used for "its": so the King James reads, "salt has lost his savour" (Matt. 5:13). "Cherubims" is found in Hebrews 9:5 instead of the correct plural "cherubim."

3. The King James Version includes errors of translation. In the seventeenth century Greek and Hebrew had only recently become subjects of serious study. At times, therefore, the translators were confronted with puzzling problems. Many of these problems were solved with skill, but others were not solved at all. For example, Mark 6:20 of the King James says that Herod put John the Baptist in prison and "observed him," but what is meant is that he "kept him safe." "Abstain from all appearance of evil" is the way the King James treats I Thess. 5:22. A more correct rendering would be: "Abstain from every form of evil."

The King James translation also inaccurately represented the text by creating distinctions in English that are not found in the Greek. Who would know that "Areopagus" and "Mars'

Hill" (Acts 17:19, 22) are different renderings of the same Greek word? The King James in Matthew 25:46 reads, "These shall go away into everlasting punishment, but the righteous into life eternal"— as though in the Greek text a distinction is made between "everlasting" and "eternal." By reading in the King James "Jeremiah" (Matt. 27:9), "Jeremias" (Matt. 16:14) and "Jeremy" (Matt. 2:14), it is possible for one to suppose that there were several Old Testament prophets with similar names instead of one "Jeremiah." On other occasions, however, the King James fails to preserve the distinctions present in the Greek text. One of the best examples of this is the persistent rendering of "hell" for both "Hades" and "Gehenna." In this way "death" and "hell" are made to be thrown into "the lake of fire" (Rev. 20:14), but a more correct translation would substitute "Hades" for "hell."

The English and American Revisions

These and other shortcomings became subjects of sharp criticism in the nineteenth century, and accordingly in February of 1870 a motion to consider a revision of the King James was passed by the Convocation of the Province of Canterbury. By May of that year proposals for the new revision had been agreed upon, and two separate committees (for Old and New Testaments) were being formed. Each committee as originally constituted was composed of twenty-seven scholars, but from time to time the exact number on the committees varied due to deaths, resignations and new appointments. These committees were joined a little later by two American committees who reviewed the work in progress and communicated their detailed suggestions to the English revisers.

The members of the committees were chosen from various denominations and possessed unimpeachable credentials of scholarship. On the English side were such giants of Biblical studies as B. F. Westcott, F. J. A. Hort, J. B. Lightfoot, R. C. Trench and A. B. Davidson. The American companies also included great names, such as Philip Schaff, J. H. Thayer, and William Henry Green.

The English companies began their work in June of 1870. The New Testament committee met on 407 days over a period of eleven years, the Old Testament committee on 792 days over a space of fifteen years. On May 17, 1881, the first installment of the long-awaited revision reached its conclusion with the issuance of the New Testament. Four years later, on May 19, 1885, the entire work was completed with publication of the Old Testament. The whole work is known as the English Revised Version.

This was essentially an English revision. American scholars had indeed cooperated in the undertaking, but in the long run the decisions of the British committees had prevailed. Divided opinions hinged mainly on differences between British and American idiom and on distinctions of spelling, with the Americans in general favoring more variations from the time-honored King James. These differences were eventually solved by compromise, with the British agreeing to print the American preferences in an attached appendix, and with the Americans agreeing that they would not issue their proposed edition until fourteen years after publication of the English revision. The result was that the American committees, which had continued to meet after the British had disbanded, put out their edition of the revision in 1901. This edition is known as the American Standard Version and differs but little from the English Revised Version, except on points of idiom, spelling, word-order, and the like. Of the two revisions, the American Standard Version is naturally preferred in this country and has enjoyed a wide circulation and approval.

Evaluation of American Standard Version

What can be said in favor of the American revision? First, the revision of 1901 is based on a Greek text which is far superior to that employed by the King James translators. It will be remembered that this shortcoming of the King James presented one urgent need for revision. Many of the earlier and most important New Testament manuscripts which were not known in 1611 were accessible to the revision committee, and accordingly its translation was based on these manuscripts. Of all the advantages of recent revisions and translations, this one is chief: an improved textual base underlying the more recent translations.

Second, the revisers have rendered their text more accurately. This is due partly to an advanced knowledge of the original languages, and partly to the unvarying ambition of the committee to produce a translation which was meticulously exact.

Third, the revisers have cleared up the misleading archaisms of the King James. A few noted examples of improvements in this respect are "spoke first to him" for "prevented him" (Matt. 17:25); "baggage" for "carriages" (Acts 21:15); "made a circuit" for "fetched a compass" (Acts 28:13); "hinder" for "let" (Rom. 1:13); "in nothing be anxious" for "be careful for nothing" (Phil. 4:6); and "grandchildren" for "nephews" (I Tim. 5:4).

Nevertheless the American revision did not escape criticism. Much of its criticism was to be expected, for people naturally resist any unfamiliar alterations made in their familiar Bibles. Other criticisms of the revision were justified. Many archaisms had been removed, but others were retained: "glory" for "praise" (Matt. 6:2); "dispute" for "discuss" (Mark 9:34); "doctor" for "teacher" (Luke 5:17); "allege" for "prove" (Acts 17:3). Not only so, but other archaisms had actually been created in order to give to the text a "Biblical" flavor. Terms as "aforetime," "would fain," "howbeit," "lest haply," "us-ward" and "you-ward" are multiplied in the American Standard Version. The net result was that what the American Standard gained in accuracy and consistency over the King James it lost in naturalness and beauty of English style. It breathed of stuffiness and lacked the plain and direct character of the primitive Biblical writings. The comment of Charles H. Spurgeon was typical of many criticisms of the new revision — "strong in Greek, weak in English." But in spite of these shortcomings the English and American revisions far excelled the illustrious King James; now it was possible for the English-speaking world to come closer than ever before to the original Bible messages.

The Revised Standard Version

The beginning of the Revised Standard Version goes back to the year of 1929. The American revision had been printed by Thomas Nelson and Sons in 1901 and had been copyrighted to safeguard against later emendations by publishers. After twenty-seven years of publication Thomas Nelson and Sons offered the expiring copyright of the American Standard Version to the In-

ternational Council of Religious Education. The International
Council accepted the copyright and appointed a committee of
scholars to consider the advisability of revising the American
Standard Version. At length it was decided that a new revision
should be made which embodied the best results of modern
scholarship and yet preserved the literary qualities of the King
James translation. By this time the country had been plunged
into the depths of a depression and funds could not be raised to
make the proposed revision a reality. It was not until 1936 that
the necessary funds were secured, and shortly afterward the
newly constituted committee began its work. By the summer of
1943 the nine members of the New Testament group, which included such well-known scholars as Edgar Goodspeed and James
Moffatt, had completed their work. They had met together over
the years on 145 days, much additional work having been done
by means of correspondence and smaller meetings of the committee. Yet because of war-time restrictions the first edition of
the New Testament did not appear until February 11, 1946.
Meanwhile the Old Testament committee continued its labors
which were finally climaxed with the publication of the complete Bible on September 30, 1952.

There are in general three reasons for the appearance of the
Revised Standard Version: (1) a recognition of the many inadequacies of the King James, (2) the failure of the English
and American revisions to overcome all of these inadequacies,
and (3) the discovery of new resources of knowledge which
would warrant, even if the recent versions had been fully ade-
quate, a new revision that includes the results of these discoveries. These new discoveries are of two classes: (1) manuscripts which confirm and at points shed additional light on the
New Testament text (cf. Chapter 7), and (2) secular papyri materials— deeds, bills of sale, formal and personal letters —which
give new information on the meanings of Greek terms current in
Biblical times.

Evaluation of Revised Standard Version

Coming a half century later, the Revised Standard Version
stands in a more advantageous position than the American
Standard Version. The new translation could fully take into

account the labors of Westcott and Hort (cf. Chapter 7), something that the earlier English and American revisions had not been able to do. Besides, the new revision committee, with a vast store of papyri at hand, at times could be more precise in its renderings. Some examples of this precision are: "delight in riches" for "deceitfulness of riches" (Matt. 13:22; Mark 4:19); "fraud" for "error" (Matt. 27:64); "after the sabbath" for "late on the sabbath" (Matt. 28:1); "until an opportune time" for "for a season" (Luke 4:13); "only Son" for "only begotten" (John 1:14); "all of them" for "both of them" (Acts 19:16); "God's field" for "God's husbandry" (I Cor. 3:9); "peddlers of God's word" for "corrupting the word of God" (II Cor. 2:17); "commonwealth" for "citizenship" (Phil. 3:20); and "in idleness" for "disorderly" (II Thess. 3:6). These examples, when studied in the light of recent research, demonstrate the high quality of translation represented in the Revised Standard Version.

Perhaps the greatest gain of the Revised Standard Version over its predecessors is its readability. The Bible, of all books, should be put in language which is understandable and easy to read. The Revised Standard seeks to recapture the beauty of the King James style in a way that is clear and pleasing to the reader. The American Standard in Matthew 21:41 crudely reads: "he will miserably destroy those miserable men"; but the Revised Standard reads: "he will put those wretches to a miserable death." The cumbersome rendering "wherefore neither thought I myself worthy to come unto thee" (ASV of Luke 7:7) becomes simply "therefore I did not presume to come to you." Many people have been reluctant to accept the Revised Standard Version, but it is unquestionably a good, usable translation.

But the Revised Standard Version also has its faults. It would be better to render "desert" for "wilderness" (Matt. 3:3); "sea monster" for "whale" (Matt. 12:40); "convict" for "convince" (John 16:8); "decided" for "determined" (Acts 11:29); "the husband of one wife" for "married only once" (I Tim. 3:2; Titus 1:6); "and then fell away" for "if they then commit apostasy" (Heb. 6:6). These are samples of a few improvements that could have been adopted by the new revision committee.

Other Recent Translations

The King James, the American Standard and the Revised Standard Versions are firmly established as the Bibles of the American people. There is every reason to believe that they will remain so in years to come. But the story of the English Bible would not be complete without mentioning a few other translations, and especially those that have been produced in the twentieth century. The Revised Standard and the American Standard Versions, even the King James itself, are revisions of previous translations: the Revised Standard a revision of the American Standard, the American Standard a revision of the King James, and the King James a revision of the Bishops' Bible. But the translations that are now to be noticed are independent translations. They were made without any regard to the language and style of translations already in existence.

1. *The Twentieth Century New Testament.* In 1955 Kenneth W. Clark published in the *Bulletin of the John Rylands Library* a notable article entitled "The Making of the Twentieth Century New Testament." It was not until the appearance of this article, based on the records kept by the translators, that the full story of *The Twentieth Century New Testament* could be told. In all about thirty people, male and female, with different vocations in life, were connected in some way with the translation project. *The Twentieth Century New Testament* was published in 1902, and besides being a good translation in itself, it is significant as a pioneer of the modern-speech versions of the century. Its chief asset, in addition to its current English, is its strong textual base, that of Westcott and Hort.

2. Weymouth's Version. In 1903 another translation in contemporary English was issued, *The New Testament in Modern Speech.* It was the work of a classical scholar, Richard Francis Weymouth, who died before the translation could be published. According to the Preface, it was a translation "made directly from the Greek" (Weymouth's own *Resultant Greek Testament*) and was "in no sense a revision." Weymouth's New Testament was revised in 1924 by James Alexander Robertson, and it is this edition that has preserved the best of Weymouth.

3. Moffatt's Version. James Moffatt was a scholar of rare talent and versatility. In his lifetime he produced an array of books

and articles on subjects of the Bible, theology, church history, church music and English literature. Moffatt is best known, however, for his translations of the Old and New Testaments. His New Testament volume appeared in 1913, entitled *The New Testament: A New Translation;* then followed his work on the Old Testament in 1924, *The Old Testament: A New Translation.* These were combined in one volume in 1926, and in 1934 Moffatt himself issued his "final" revision of the entire work.

The Moffatt translation has enjoyed wide acclaim. At times its simple and direct phraseology is incomparable. No one can read Moffatt's version of I Corinthians 13 without being struck with awe. But Moffatt's translation has some genuine weak points. The New Testament portion is based on the Greek text of Hermann von Soden, a newly published text when Moffatt undertook his translation. Since that time, however, the von Soden text has proved to be defective, which has left Moffatt's New Testament disappointing in this respect. The way Moffatt has handled the Old Testament text has been sharply criticized also. It was Moffatt's opinion that "the traditional or 'Massoretic' text of the Old Testament . . . is often desperately corrupt." Thus in the introductory pages of his translation he explains to the reader how often — "nearly every page" — it has been necessary for him to emend and re-organize the Old Testament text. Even Genesis 1:1 is rearranged, and Genesis 2:4a becomes the first verse in Moffatt's translation. This task of textual correction is pursued in the New Testament as well. In the Gospel of John, for example, many sections of material are rearranged; to cite two illustrations, John 7:15-24 follows 5:47, and chapters 15 and 16 follow 13:31. Whatever motives Moffatt had in mind, such emendations are not in the province of the translator. It is the task of the translator to represent as accurately as possible the best text available to him as attested by the best authorities.

4. Goodspeed's Version. The late Edgar J. Goodspeed of the University of Chicago published his version in 1923. Goodspeed called it *The New Testament: An American Translation* because he felt that a modern-speech translation was needed in American idiom. A little later, in 1927, *The Complete Bible: An American Translation* came off the press. The Old Testament was not the work of Goodspeed, however, but was due to the labors of J. M.

Powis Smith and others. Goodspeed's New Testament has been well received. The Greek text underlying it is better than Moffatt's, being based on the edition of Westcott and Hort. The Goodspeed New Testament is a valuable translation in current English.

5. Phillips' Version. In 1958 J. B. Phillips' *New Testament in Modern Speech* was published. Prior to this time, from 1947 to 1957, it had been issued in separate installments. From the first Phillips' translation has had much appeal. It divides the subject-matter of the New Testament books into small parts and commends itself to the ordinary reader because *it makes sense*. A number of people have objected to Phillips' version on the grounds that it is a paraphrase. But a paraphrase is not necessarily bad, any more than a literal, word-for-word translation is always good. What is important is that a translation not become a commentary; and it would not be fair to say that J. B. Phillips is a commentator rather than a translator.

6. The New English Bible. Until very recently the history of the English Bible was a history of revisions. Since 1961, with the appearance of the New English Bible, this is no longer true. The publication of the New English Bible coincided with the three hundred and fiftieth anniversary of the King James Version, but its historic importance lies in the fact that it is a complete departure from the respected ancestry of the Tyndale-King James tradition. Other private translations, of course, had done this, but not a translation produced by a group of representative Protestant scholars.

As one examines the New English Bible, his first impression is that it is really new. Its textual base is new, neither that of Westcott-Hort or Nestle or any other. Like the Revised Standard Version its text is eclectic in nature, but unlike the Revised Standard it often parts company with the most weighty textual authorities (cf. John 1:18; 3:13; Rom. 8:28; Eph. 1:1).

The New English Bible also embodies a new principle of translation. The older revisions, especially the Revised Version of 1881, were scrupulously literal: the translators insisted that a version was "faithful" only if it met the word-for-word requirement. But the New English Bible, following the precedent set by recent private translations and the Revised Standard Version, has broken away from the word-for-word principle in the interest of replacing "Greek constructions and idioms by those of contemporary English." The New English Bible, then, is a sense-for-sense translation rather than a word-for-word translation.

Any translation that abandons the word-for-word principle leaves itself open to attack — and the New English Bible has proved to be no exception. The point of concern, however, should be how *accurate* the New English Bible is in conveying the Biblical message. John 1:1 may be taken as an illustration. The New English Bible reads: "When all things began, the Word already was. The Word dwelt with God, and what God was, the Word was." Here is a very beautiful and accurate translation, but it is not one that is word-for-word.

There are dangers, of course, in this kind of translation, for it is very easy to slip over into the role of the commentator. Not a few times, sometimes unavoidably, has the New English Bible fallen into this fallacy, but taken as a whole it represents an honest effort to state in unambiguous language what the New Testament meant to its first readers. Therefore, any evaluation of the New English Bible in general should begin with the principles of translation as stated in its Introduction, and any criticism of it in particular should hinge on the degree of success with which the meaning of each paragraph is expressed.

As one would expect, the language of the New English Bible is different. The translators have tried to use "the natural vocabulary, constructions, and rhythms of contemporary speech." In this respect it has largely measured up to its intentions. But for the American reader its choice of words at times is unfortunate. Reading through the New Testament one is able to accumulate quite a list of non-American terms and expressions. In the Gospel of Mark the following occur: "make away with him" (3:6); "young corn" (4:6); "meal-tub" (4:21); "took to their heels" (5:14); "fell foul of him" (6:4); "farmsteads" (6:56); "rounded on him" (10:48); "tethered" (11:2); and "truckle" (12:14). Some of these expressions are as difficult to the American reader as the Elizabethan English of the older versions. For this reason, in addition to others that will vary from person to person, it is not likely that for the American reader the New English Bible will supplant the Revised Standard Version as the most popular recent translation.

Summary

No one translation is infallible. With the advance of time it was inevitable that revisions would have to be made of the classic King James Version: (1) its translation was based on manuscripts of late (instead of early) dates; (2) it contained obsolete expressions which were often misleading; and (3) it did not always represent an exact translation of the original tongues. The English Revised and American Standard Versions have largely met the needs for revision, especially in providing translations which are based on earlier and more reliable manuscripts. But changes of time and other discoveries have made more recent revisions and translations desirable. The twentieth century has witnessed a surge of new translations. All of them have their faults, of course, but some of them are especially good and can be of great help to the Bible reader. One of these is the Revised Standard Version — a translation that undoubtedly can be improved upon, but nevertheless one that deserves the attention and use of Bible students. If in no other way, it can be profitably used by comparison with the King James and American Standard Versions. The Scripture references cited in this chapter should be studied carefully by comparison of the various translations. In this way the individual Bible student can come to his own conclusion as to the most useful translation for him; and at the same time, it is hoped, can come to see the value of all the translations.

For Consideration

1. List some of the basic weaknesses of the King James Version that called for a new revision.
2. Relate briefly something of the background of the English revision. In what years were the following first published: (1) N.T. revision, (2) O.T. revision, and (3) American Standard Version.
3. What brought about the issuance of the American Standard Version? How would you distinguish between the English Revised Version and the American Standard Version?

4. What are some of the chief merits of the American Standard Version? List some of its criticisms also.
5. Review in brief the main factors leading up to the publication of the Revised Standard Version.
6. What are the main strengths and weaknesses of the Revised Standard Version?
7. Discuss the modern speech translations. How do they differ from the American Standard Versions?

13

"My Words Will Not Pass Away"

Tracing the Bible down through the centuries presents the human side of how we got the Bible. From a different standpoint, the story of how we got the Bible begins and ends with God. God is Light, the Source of Light, both physical and spiritual. Ultimately, then, the question of how we got the Bible leads us to the throne of God.

In Mark 13:31 Jesus said: "Heaven and earth will pass away, but my words will not pass away." Here Jesus makes two claims. First, He claims that His words are divine: the world will pass away but His words will not; therefore, His words are not from the world. Second, because His words are divine, Jesus claims that His words will stand forever.

"My Words"

The claim made by Jesus for His words, that they are divine, is the claim the Bible as a whole makes for itself. The apostle Paul wrote: "All Scripture is inspired by God and profitable for teaching, for reproof, for correction, and for training in righteousness, that the man of God may be complete, equipped for every good work" (II Tim. 4:16-17). The term "Scripture" is here used in a special sense, referring to the canonical writings of the Old Testament. It was Paul's belief that the Old Testament writings had come from God, literally, were *God-breathed.*

In a similar passage another apostle said: "And we have the prophetic word made more sure. You will do well to pay attention to this as to a lamp shining in a dark place, until the day dawns and the morning star rises in your hearts. First of all you must understand this, that no prophecy of scripture is a matter of one's own interpretation, because no prophecy ever came by the impulse of man, but men moved by the Holy Spirit spoke from God" (II Peter 1:19-21). The Old Testament writers, said Peter, did not invent or devise the messages of their books. What each of them said and wrote was due to an influence outside themselves: they spoke from God as the Holy Spirit guided them. Each of these passages plainly affirms that the Old Testament is of divine origin.

If the Old Testament prophets were inspired by God, is it conceivable that New Testament men, including the Savior and His apostles, would possess less inspiration than they? We expect to find, therefore, an inspiration in the New Testament at least equal to that of the Old. And this is what we do find. The Lord often contrasted his teachings with Moses' law (cf. Matt. 5:27-48), leaving the unavoidable impression that a greater than Moses had come. His chosen apostles were endowed with such authority that whatever they required on earth became a requirement in heaven (Matt. 16:18). The church at Corinth was expected to acknowledge that what the apostle Paul wrote to them was "a command of the Lord" (I Cor. 14:37). And the early New Testament churches did acknowledge such apostolic authority. They received the words of the apostles "not as the word of men but as what it really is, the word of God" (I Thess. 2:13).

It may be objected that this is reasoning in a circle, that inspiration is assumed in order to prove inspiration. But this is not true. It is assumed, however, that the men who wrote the Bible were honest men and were of a sound mind. If they were sane and sound-minded, they would not be susceptible to fanciful visions and hallucinations; if they were honest, they would not intentionally deceive.

Much of the uniqueness of the Bible rests on its unique claims. Permitting it to speak for itself, the Bible claims to be from God. This claim comes from honest, straight-thinking men and deserves consideration. The claim does not authenticate the truthfulness of the claim, but the contents of the Bible, with its theme of salvation and its strong moral fiber, support it. Jesus' ethical principles, for example, are either human or divine. The Bible says that they are divine, a claim not preposterous in view of its lofty standards of morality. The *claims* of the Bible plus the *contents* of the Bible equal a *convincing case* for the Bible as the inspired Word of God.

"Will Not Pass Away"

Jesus promised that His words would not pass away. Divine Providence through the centuries has been working in many ways to fulfill this promise. Viewing the situation in the twentieth century, many evidences can be observed which show that the Lord is preserving His Word.

1. The quantity of materials available on the Bible text. The number of textual documents, including manuscripts and versions, is so vast that it practically defies calculation — a conservative guess would be at least 20,000. Of these, as we have seen, some 4,500 alone are manuscripts of the New Testament. It is interesting to compare this figure with the manuscripts by which the principal Greek and Roman writings have come down to us. The History of Thucydides, for example, which was written about 400 B.C., is available today on the basis of eight manuscripts; while the few books that remain of the Roman historian Tacitus (*c*. 100 A.D.) have survived on the margin of two manuscripts. In other words, the great classical writings are transmitted to the present day by no more than a handful of manuscripts. This being true, and since no one really questions the textual foundations of the classics, why should a mist of doubt prevail over the Bible text? If any book from ancient times has descended to us without substantial loss or alteration, it is the Bible. The Bible is the best-attested book from the ancient world! This has prompted Sir Frederic Kenyon to say: "The number of manuscripts of the New Testament, of early translations from it, and of quotations from it in the oldest writers of the Church, is so large that it is practically certain that the true reading of every doubtful passage is preserved in some one or other of these ancient authorities. This can be said of no other ancient book in the world."[1]

2. The quality of materials available on the Bible text. Infor-

---

[1]Sir Frederic Kenyon, *Our Bible and the Ancient Manuscripts*. Revised by A. W. Adams. (New York: Harper and Brothers, 1958), p. 55.

mation on the Bible text is not only abundant but is reliable as well. The celebrated Vatican and Sinaitic Manuscripts are only two centuries removed from the close of the apostolic age, and even this period is partially filled in by recently discovered papyrus documents. If there were no papyri, the text of the New Testament would still stand in a remarkably advantageous position. This can be seen by further reference to the classics mentioned above. The two manuscripts of Tacitus' works are of late date, one from the ninth century and the other from the eleventh; and none of the manuscripts of Thucydides, except for fragments, date any earlier than the tenth century. Copies of Thucydides are thus about 1300 years later than the date of their original composition, yet no effort is made to discount these copies in spite of such a wide interval of time. These examples cited from the classics are not isolated cases, for the fact is that the vast majority of writings from ancient times have been preserved on late-date manuscripts. In contrast, our New Testament text rests on manuscripts which are very near to the date of their original composition. The text of the New Testament, as compared with other ancient books, holds a unique and enviable rank.

Summary

Perhaps it is wise now to summarize the main points in each of the preceding chapters in order that the essential features of the Bible's history may be permanently fixed in our minds.

1. For the history of the Bible the most important writing materials are leather, papyrus and vellum. Leather was principally used in the Old Testament period, while the New Testament books were undoubtedly first penned on papyrus. About the fourth century A.D. papyrus was replaced by vellum, with the result that practically all the New Testament manuscripts today are inscribed on vellum.

2. Our Bible is an amazing collection of books. The various books of the Bible often have been differently but logically arranged. The Bible was originally written in three languages: Hebrew, Aramaic and Greek. The New Testament was written in Greek; the Old Testament was written in Hebrew, with some sections in Aramaic.

3. Manuscripts of the New Testament are of two classes: uncials and cursives. Cursives are those written in long-hand style, while uncials are those found in large, capital letters. Of the two, the uncials are earlier and are the more important as authorities on the New Testament text. The three famous uncials are: the Vatican, the Sinaitic and the Alexandrian Manuscripts.

4. Two other important manuscripts are Codex Ephraem and Codex Bezae. Additional aid on the Bible text comes from many ancient versions and from numerous Scripture quotations made by the early Fathers. Thus there are three sources of information on the New Testament text: (1) the manuscripts, (2) the versions, and (3) the quotations from the early church writers.

5. It was inevitable that transcription mistakes would appear in the production of copies. The task of Textual Criticism is to detect these mistakes and mark them off from the pure text. With a wealth of information at his hand, and following exact principles, the textual critic is able to do this with a high degree of precision.

6. Textual variants are of different types and degrees of importance. Most variants are obvious slips made by the scribe and present no problem. Others are of no consequence to our present text because they are not found in the most reliable manuscripts. Some represent substantial variation, but in this number no unique Biblical teaching or divine command is involved.

7. Our present New Testament text is a reconstructed Greek text. Westcott and Hort are largely responsible for this reconstruction. Many enlightening discoveries have been made in the last eighty years, but all of them confirm the Westcott-Hort type of text. New materials which have turned up make the text of the Bible more and more secure.

8. The work of the Massoretes and other early Jewish scribes has resulted in a carefully copied edition of the Old Testament text. The recently discovered Dead Sea Scrolls, especially the two Isaiah scrolls, give unquestioned support to the reliability of our accepted Old Testament text.

9. The term canon applies to those books that are included in the Bible as authoritative Scripture. Separate books became a

part of the canon gradually. Much clear-cut and indisputable evidence exists as to which books were and were not accounted as Scripture.

10. "The Apocrypha" usually refers to a group of about fifteen books not included in our Old Testament. The Apocrypha represent different types of literature: (1) historical, (2) legendary, (3) prophetic, and (4) ethical. Many sound reasons can be given for not including these doubtful books in our Bibles, the chief reason being that they have never been accepted in the Hebrew canon of the Old Testament.

11. William Tyndale is the true father of the English Bible. He was the first to translate the New Testament in English based on a Greek text. He himself suffered martydom, but his ambition to put the Bible in the hands of the people lived on, eventually resulting in the appearance of the illustrious King James Version.

12. Increasing knowledge of the Bible text, and related matters, has made it necessary in recent years to revise the King James translation. The main revisions have been the American Standard and the Revised Standard Versions. Each of these translations has its faults, but each also has its great advantages. The most important advantage of recent translations is that they are based on early manuscripts and thus stand closer to the original inspired message.

Conclusion

It is a comforting and reassuring thought to know that Jesus' words will be preserved through the ages. This promise of Jesus has been tested by centuries and has not failed. "The grass withers, and the flowers fall, but the word of the Lord abides forever" (I Peter 1:24-25).

The Word of God is accessible to English-speaking people in many translations. Some translations are good, others are better. None of the major translations are so bad, and no Greek text is so faulty, as to lead one from "the Lamb of God who takes away the sin of the world." Improvements of translation, to be sure, ought to be welcomed and appreciated. But the important thing is that the individual *use* the translation he favors. Because the modern farmer has a variety of new equipment, this does not guarantee for him a successful crop. The equipment must be used. Likewise, in a period where God's grace abounds in the supply of new and better helps for Bible study, let us not presume that the presence of the equipment can substitute for the use of it. May God grant that we shall continue to be a people of one book, and that book the Bible.

FOR CONSIDERATION

1. List two important passages which claim that the Old Testament is inspired. What evidence is there to show that the apostles in New Testament times also possessed inspiration?
2. Is inspiration assumed in order to prove inspiration? If not, what is assumed?
3. How does the quantity of evidence on the New Testament text compare with the quantity available for other ancient books?
4. Evaluate, in brief, the quality of evidence that bears on the Bible text. Is the Bible truly the best-attested book from the ancient world? How does this affect your faith in God and in the authority of the Bible?

A SHORT BIBLIOGRAPHY

Bruce, F. F. *Are the New Testament Documents Reliable?* Grand Rapids: Wm. B. Eerdmans Publishing Company, 1954.

————. *The Books and the Parchments.* Los Angeles: Fleming H. Revell Company, 1950.

————. *The English Bible.* New York: Oxford University Press, 1961.

————. *Second Thoughts on the Dead Sea Scrolls.* Grand Rapids: Wm. B. Eerdmans Publishing Company, 1956.

Burrows, Millar. *The Dead Sea Scrolls.* New York: The Viking Press, 1955.

Finegan, Jack. *Light from the Ancient Past.* Princeton: Princeton University Press, 1949.

Gregory, Caspar Rene. *Canon and Text of the New Testament.* New York: Charles Scribner's Sons, 1920.

Herklots, H. G. G. *How Our Bible Came to Us.* New York: Oxford University Press, 1954.

Kenyon, Sir Frederic G. *Handbook to the Textual Criticism of the New Testament.* Second edition, reprinted. Grand Rapids: Wm. B. Eerdmans Publishing Company, n.d.

————. *Our Bible and the Ancient Manuscripts.* Revised by A. W. Adams. New York: Harper and Brothers, 1958.

————. *The Story of the Bible.* New York: E. P. Dutton & Co., Inc., 1937.

————. *The Text of the Greek Bible.* London: Duckworth, 1937.

Lightfoot, Joseph Barber. *On a Fresh Revision of the English New Testament.* Third Edition. London: Macmillan and Co., 1891.

Price, Ira Maurice. *The Ancestry of Our English Bible.* Third Revised Edition by William A. Irwin and Allen P. Wikgren. New York: Harper and Brothers, 1956.

Roberts, Bleddyn J. *The Old Testament Text and Versions.* Cardiff: University of Wales Press, 1951.

Robinson, H. Wheeler (ed.). *The Bible in Its Ancient and English Versions.* Oxford: Clarendon Press, 1940.

Smyth, J. Paterson. *How We Got Our Bible*. New York: James Pott and Company, 1899.

Souter, Alexander. *The Text and Canon of the New Testament*. Revised by C. S. C. Williams. London: Gerald Duckworth and Company, Ltd., 1954.

Tregelles, Samuel Prideaux. *An Account of the Printed Text of the Greek New Testament*. London: Samuel Bagster and Sons, 1854.

Westcott, B. F. *A General Survey of the History of the Canon of the New Testament*. Fifth Edition. Cambridge: University Press, 1881.

Westcott, B. F. and F. J. A. Hort. *The New Testament in the Original Greek*. Introduction and Appendix. Cambridge: University Press, 1881.

Wurthwein, Ernst. *The Text of the Old Testament*. Translated by Peter R. Ackroyd. New York: The Macmillan Company, 1957.

Index